TUBMAN TRAVELS

32 Underground Railroad Journeys on Delmarva

TUBMAN TRAVELS

32 Underground Railroad Journeys on Delmarva

A Secrets of the Eastern Shore Guide

BY JIM DUFFY

Published by Secrets of the Eastern Shore
Cambridge, Maryland

Publishing Services by Happy Self Publishing
www.happyselfpublishing.com

Cover art created for the book by
Lisa Krentel, used with permission.

ISBN: 978-0-9978005-1-7

Also by Jim Duffy:
Eastern Shore Road Trips
27 One-Day Adventures on Delmarva

More Eastern Shore Stories & Travels:
SecretsoftheEasternShore.com
Facebook.com/SecretsoftheEasternShore

Questions, Comments, Suggestions:
SecretsoftheEasternShore@gmail.com
443.477.4490

Contents

INTRODUCTION

I got to talking one day with a woman who was quite interested in the stories of Harriet Tubman and the Underground Railroad. She and a friend had been thinking about taking a road trip to visit Tubman sites on the Eastern Shore of Maryland, where I live, and across the way in Delaware.

One worry held them back: "What would we actually *see*?"

It's a great question, actually, and it's what this book is all about. The Underground Railroad is a different kind of travel experience. At more traditional historic sites—let's use Monticello as an example—visitors get to walk through the very rooms where Thomas Jefferson walked and ogle all kinds of artifacts and gadgets straight from his life.

There are no Monticellos on the Underground Railroad. No trace remains of the cabin where Harriet Tubman was born. No one knows for sure exactly where it used to stand. The cabin where Frederick Douglass was born disappeared so long ago that Douglass himself had trouble finding the spot in his later years.

Following the Underground Railroad here on the Delmarva Peninsula, you are more likely to end up at the mouth a creek, in a stand of trees, or along a stretch of marshland. The stories that unfolded on these landscapes will more likely than not have a bit of uncertainty to them. You are going to come across the words *might* and *perhaps* and *probably* quite a bit in the pages that follow.

This is the nature of the topic. Slaves on the run did not bother to record the turns they took or the places they hid while crossing through hundreds of miles of unfamiliar territory with bloodhounds and bounty hunters on their trail. The station masters and conductors who helped them along the way did everything they could to stay in the shadows, too.

And so traveling the Underground Railroad is different. That is going to be true regardless of whether you plan to actually hit the road or you are more of an armchair traveler. Either way, it's best to set out here with a fresh set of eyes, open to new ways of encountering the past and imagining the lives of people from times gone by.

The stories you will encounter along the way are, as far as I'm concerned, as moving and inspiring as any in human history. They revolve around the quest for freedom from bondage, of course, but as you delve into them you'll see that they are also about the whole array of emotions at the heart of life—love, death, birth, heartbreak, God, evil, loss, courage, family, and more.

Here's hoping that this book helps you get in touch with those stories in the fullest possible measure.

Happy wandering,

Jim Duffy
Secrets of the Eastern Shore

A Note on Organization

This book is organized geographically, so that travelers can follow along chapter by chapter in the book while traveling across Maryland's Eastern Shore and into Delaware. I tried to make it as convenient as possible for travelers to create daytrips out of two or three or more chapters, all right in the same vicinity.

Roughly half of the "journeys" here focus on key events in the lives of Harriet Tubman and Frederick Douglass. The book's geographic organization means that some of those stories appear out of chronological order. I have done my best to make sure each chapter in this book can be read as a stand-alone piece.

But if you would prefer to read the stories of Tubman and Douglass in chronological order from youth into adulthood, here is how to do that:

TUBMAN STORIES IN CHRONOLOGICAL ORDER

DOUGLASS STORIES IN CHRONOLOGICAL ORDER

BONUS MATERIALS

As a thank you for giving this book a chance, I have prepared some bonus materials and loaded them up on the Secrets of the Eastern Shore website for you to download. These materials can be found at:

SecretsoftheEasternShore.com/tubman-extras

The materials include:

AFRICAN AMERICAN HISTORY SITES

The Delmarva Peninsula is full of sites that speak to the broader African American experience but are not directly related to the Underground Railroad. This resource lists and briefly describes dozens of those sites in the geographic region covered by this book—the middle and upper parts of the Eastern Shore of Maryland, the upper half of the state of Delaware, and the Seaford area of Southern Delaware.

DETAILED DRIVING DIRECTIONS

Each chapter in this book begins with a visual geographic overview of where the story at hand is situated on or near the Delmarva Peninsula. Where possible, each chapter also includes addresses that can be plugged into your favorite device for generating maps and directions.

I learned in doing my previous book that there are a good number of people who don't like using such devices. For those readers, I have prepared a detailed set of driving directions that begins at Chapter 1 and runs in order from site to site through Chapter 32.

Again, you can download these bonus materials at:
SecretsoftheEasternShore.com/tubman-extras

Keeping Names Straight

If you get confused while reading this book about who is who in Harriet Tubman's family, come back here to find a quick answer.

THE GRANDMOTHER
- **Modesty Green** (owned in slavery by Atthow Pattison)

THE PARENTS
- **Ben Ross** (owned in slavery by Anthony C. Thompson)
- **Harriet "Rit" Ross** (inherited by and then owned in slavery by the Brodess family)

THE SIBLINGS
(All owned by the Brodess family before the incidents of sale or freedom mentioned below.)
- **Linah Ross** (b. 1808)
  Sold to the South and never seen again

- **Mariah Ritty Ross** (b. 1811)
  Sold to the South and never seen again
- **Soph Ross** (b. 1813)
  Sold to the South and never seen again
- **Robert Ross** (b. 1816)
  Found freedom in the North, changed name to John Stewart
- **Araminta Ross** (b. 1822)
  Changed her name to Harriet Tubman in her early 20s; found freedom in the North and became Underground Railroad conductor
- **Ben Ross** (b. 1823)
  Found freedom in the North, changed name to James Stewart
- **Rachel Ross** (b. 1825)
  Never escaped slavery, died of unknown causes at estimated age of 35
- **Henry Ross** (b. 1830)
  Found freedom in the North, changed name to William H. Stewart
- **Moses Ross** (b. 1832)
  Found freedom in the North, but drops out of historical record almost immediately after that and later fate unknown

1: Modesty on the Choptank

Cambridge, Maryland

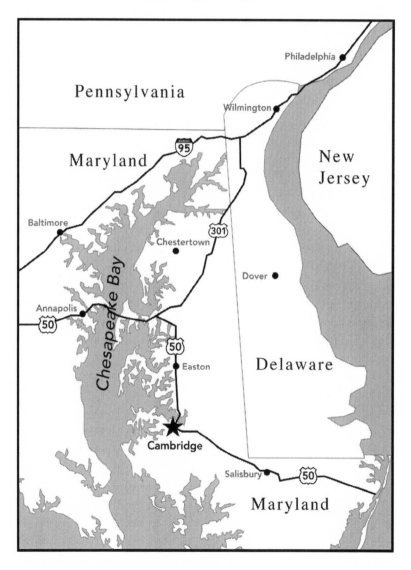

BIG PICTURE
The View from the Lighthouse

The Choptank River Lighthouse didn't exist in slavery times. It's not a place Harriet Tubman or some other hero of the Underground Railroad might have visited. So why start here?

The lighthouse stands on the Choptank River at Long Wharf Park in Cambridge, Maryland, its bright red roof gleaming in the sun at the end of a long pier lined with traditional Eastern Shore workboats. Stroll that pier, then climb the stairs and meander around the little deck that circles the six-sided structure.

The views from this lighthouse are timeless. The Choptank is a big piece of water here, nearly two miles across. Stay to your left when you get up on that deck, then keep your eyes to the left as you make your way around. That's where the river runs eventually into the Chesapeake Bay, which runs in turn into the Atlantic Ocean and then out into the whole wide world.

Traffic on the river nowadays is a mix of watermen at work and sailors at play. In slavery times, however, the Choptank was the U.S. Route 50 of its day, an economic superhighway connecting this otherwise isolated outpost in the midst of Maryland's Eastern Shore with cities up and down the East Coast, as well as to trade markets across the Atlantic Ocean.

Time to put your imagination to work: Bring up in your mind's eye the picture of an old-school tall ship, and then place that ship off on the western horizon. Can you see the sails in the distance?

STORY
Modesty on the Choptank

All manner of cargo made its way up and down the Choptank River in the 1700s, including, alas, human cargo. The river was not an especially active route for the big slave ships, but they came up this way now and again in the years before the United States outlawed the international slave trade in 1807.

In the latter part of the 1700s, a boat came up this river with a captive woman from the Ashanti region of West Africa on board. We have no record of which vessel this might have been, so there is guesswork involved in thinking about her journey. Oftentimes back then, Africans brought to the Eastern Shore came by way of the West Indies, where they may have spent months or years toiling in slavery. But there are thin threads of oral history indicating that this particular woman might have arrived straight from the area we know today as Ghana and the Ivory Coast.

Did the slave ship that brought her across the ocean sail all the way into Cambridge? It's possible. It's also possible that the ship stopped in some other port on the Chesapeake Bay. Perhaps this Ashanti woman was sold at auction there and eventually came up the Choptank aboard a smaller vessel.

We don't know this woman's given name, her age, or anything at all about her life before she was forced from her homeland. What we can say for sure is that her journey across the ocean was an unspeakable ordeal. From the deck at the lighthouse, it's easy to imagine those sails on the horizon, but it's nearly impossible to imagine what that Ashanti woman—and millions more just like her—went through while crossing the ocean.

One historian after another uses the same phrase to describe the way slaves stood in the dark holds of slave ships—they were "stacked like books on a shelf." There were no bathroom facilities down there. People relieved themselves where they stood. Perhaps they were able to make use of so-called "necessary bowls," but perhaps not. Those who got seasick had nowhere to go, either. They vomited where they stood, in the midst of all that filth and misery. The stench that wafted up out of these holds was so foul that crews aboard merchant vessels did everything they could to avoid getting stuck downwind of a slave ship.

The way it worked on most ships, slaves were dragged up on deck twice a day, chained in pairs. They were given a bit of water and a little soup. They were also forced to get a little exercise, so as to keep up their muscles and thereby prop up their value to potential buyers.

Infectious diseases ran wild. At least one of every eight people in the hold died during an average trip. The bodies of the fallen were tossed overboard without ceremony. This Ashanti woman was among the survivors when her ship came up the Choptank.

Make your way around to the other side of that lighthouse deck until you spot a pretty little finger of water off to the right. That is Cambridge Creek, it runs into the heart of town, which is where the vessel carrying that Ashanti woman might well have docked.

When she emerged, perhaps still in chains, she would have found herself in the midst of a bustling little port dominated by shipyards full of clanging hammers and roaring fires and creaking timbers and screaming dockworkers. The noise and chaos in that shipyard must have seemed beyond strange to this Ashanti woman.

The famed abolitionist and orator Frederick Douglass, who was born into slavery just 20 or so miles from here, toiled during the 1830s in the shipyards of Baltimore's Fells Point neighborhood. In his *Narrative of the Life of Frederick Douglass*, he recalls what his first experience of a shipyard was like when he was just starting out as a glorified gofer.

In entering the shipyard, my orders from Mr. Gardner were to do whatever the carpenters commanded me to do. ... My situation was a most trying one. At times I needed a dozen pair of hands. I was called a dozen ways in the space of a single minute. Three or four voices would strike my ear at the same moment.

It was—"Fred, come help me to cant this timber here."—"Fred, come carry this timber yonder."—"Fred, bring that roller here."—"Fred, go get a fresh can of water."—"Fred, come help saw off the end of this timber."—"Fred, go quick, and get the crowbar."—"Fred, hold on the end of this fall."—"Fred, go to the blacksmith's shop, and get a new punch."—"Hurra, Fred! Run and bring me a cold chisel."—"I say, Fred, bear a hand, and get up a fire as quick as lightning under that steam-box."—"Halloo, nigger! Come turn this grindstone."—"Come, come! Move, move! And bowse this time forward."—"I say, darky, blast your eyes, why don't you heat up some pitch?"—"Halloo! Halloo! Halloo!" (Three voices at the same time.) "Come here!—Go there!—Hold on where you are. Damn you, if you move, I'll knock your brains out!"

Here on the Eastern Shore, the Ashanti woman would come to be known as Modesty Green. Legally, Modesty was the property of a farmer named Atthow Pattison. She would give birth to a child named Harriet, or "Rit." Another thin thread of family lore has it that the father of that girl was a white man, but there is no telling for sure.

When Atthow Pattison died in 1797, Modesty and Rit would become the property of his daughter, Elizabeth. At this point, all traces of Modesty disappear from surviving records. We know nothing, really, about her life here. We don't even know when or how she died.

What we do know is that her daughter Rit would eventually become the property of Elizabeth's daughter, Mary, who married one man who died young and then married another man after that. This second husband owned a slave named Ben Ross.

Rit and Ben fell in love and got married. They had nine children together. The one in the middle was a girl named Araminta, or "Minty." In time, the world would come to know this granddaughter of that Ashanti woman by another name, Harriet Tubman.

TESTIMONY
Aboard a Slave Ship

Olaudah Equiano was kidnapped in West Africa at age 11 and sold to slave traders, who forced him to endure the voyage across the ocean aboard a slave ship in the mid-1750s. This scene from his book, *The Interesting Life of Olaudah Equiano, or Gustavus Vassa, The African*, begins in Africa, as he arrives in chains on the shores of the Atlantic.

The first object which saluted my eyes was ... a slave ship, which was then riding at anchor, and waiting for its cargo. [This] filled me with astonishment, which was soon converted into terror when I was carried on board. [I looked around the ship and saw] a multitude of black people of every description chained together, every one of their countenances expressing dejection and sorrow....

I was soon put down under the decks, and there I received such a salutation in my nostrils as I had never experienced in my life: so that, with the loathsomeness of the stench, and crying together, I became so sick and low that I was not able to eat, nor had I the least desire to taste anything. I now wished for the last friend, death, to relieve me; but soon, to my grief, two of the white men offered me eatables; and, on my refusing to eat, one of them held me fast by the hands, and laid me across I think the windlass, and tied my feet, while the other flogged me severely....

[During the voyage that followed], it became absolutely pestilential [in the hold]. The closeness of the place, and the heat of the climate, added to the number in the ship, which was so crowded that each had scarcely room to turn himself, almost suffocated us. This produced copious perspirations, so that the air soon became unfit for respiration, from a variety of loathsome smells, and brought on a sickness among the slaves, of which many died.... The shrieks of the women, and the groans of the dying, rendered the whole a scene of horror almost inconceivable....

I began to hope [that death] would soon put an end to my miseries.

Later, the ship carrying Equiano lands in a busy harbor in the West Indies.

Many merchants and planters now came on board, though it was in the evening. They put us in separate parcels, and examined us attentively. They also made us jump, and pointed to the land, signifying we were to go there. We thought by this we should be eaten by these ugly men....

We were not many days in the [custody of a merchant] before we were sold after their usual manner, which is this:—On a signal given ... the buyers rush at once into the yard where the slaves are confined and make choice of that parcel they like best. The noise and clamour with which this is attended, and the eagerness visible in the countenances of the buyers, serve not a little to increase the apprehensions of the terrified Africans....

In this manner, without scruple, are relations and friends separated, most of them never to see each other again. I remember in the vessel in which I was brought over ... there were several brothers, who, in the sale, were sold in different lots; and it was very moving on this occasion to see and hear their cries at parting.

CONNECTIONS

Here at the outset I focused on Modesty Green and her journey to the Eastern Shore because that marks the start of the family that would eventually give birth to Harriet Tubman. But this is not the only Underground Railroad story to think about while making your way around the deck of the Choptank River Lighthouse.

- A little way up High Street in Cambridge stands the Dorchester County Courthouse, site of the very first escape that Harriet Tubman helped to engineer. That story is in Chapter 2.
- Also that way, at 111 High Street, is a house where a slave named Samuel Green, Jr. escaped. The story of his family is in Chapter 11.
- Across the river in Talbot County is the farm where a slave named Moses Viney escaped. The story of "The Other Moses" is in Chapter 17.
- Upriver, beyond the Malkus Bridge, the Choptank takes a turn to the north and then narrows gradually as it runs near or through East New Market, Poplar Neck, Preston, Denton, and Greensboro. Those place names are going to pop up over and over again in the pages that follow, as countless runaways followed the banks of this river while making their way north to freedom.
- Also that way is the mouth of Tuckahoe Creek. The famed orator and abolitionist Frederick Douglass

was born into slavery on the shores of that creek. The story of his childhood there is in Chapter 19.

TRAVEL RESOURCES

The **Choptank River Lighthouse** is open to the public daily between May 1 and Oct. 31. Off-season tours are available by appointment.
- High and Water streets, Cambridge, Maryland
- ChoptankRiverLighthouse.org; Facebook.com/ChoptankRiverLighthouse; 410.463.2653

The first three stops in this book are in or near downtown Cambridge, where there are a good number of shops, restaurants, and attractions. Information about things to do and places to go while visiting the town is available from **Dorchester County Tourism**.
- Dorchester Visitor Center, 2 Rose Hill Place, Cambridge, Maryland
- VisitDorchester.org; Facebook.com/DorchesterCounty; 410.228.1000

The **Harriet Tubman Underground Railroad Byway** runs through both Dorchester and Caroline counties in Maryland and then on into Delaware.
- Maryland: HarrietTubmanByway.org; Facebook.com/HarrietTubmanByway; 410.228.1000
- Delaware: TubmanBywayDelaware.org

2: Flight from the Auction Block

Cambridge, Maryland

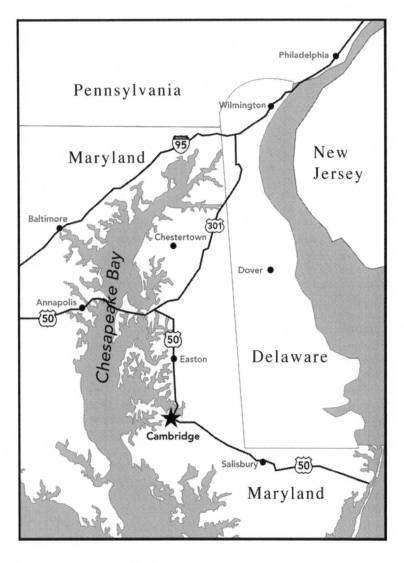

BIG PICTURE
The Maritime Life

The walk back from the Choptank River Lighthouse, where we left off in the last chapter, will take you onto a long pier lined with "deadrise" workboats owned by local watermen. If you're lucky, you might pass by as one or more of these watermen go about their trade—unloading bushels of crabs, perhaps, or baiting lines for another run come dawn of the next day.

The presence of these vessels along the promenade leading up to a prominent tourist destination in Cambridge, Maryland is a statement of civic pride in the centuries-old traditions of maritime life hereabouts. The work these men do aboard their boats today is the modern-day version of the day-to-day life of a free black man named John Bowley back in the 1840s.

The stories we hear of slavery tend to be set on farm fields more often than not, with workers toiling away at sowing or harvesting or managing the affairs in a plantation mansion or smaller farmhouse. Here on the Eastern Shore in John Bowley's time, a substantial minority of slaves and free blacks were assigned to work the water instead, transporting timber and building ships. It was boom times for the local shipbuilding industry back then.

Bowley worked in shipbuilding, and as a blacksmith. He was part owner of a schooner, too. That work put him square in the middle of the commercial superhighway that ran along the Choptank River, out to the Chesapeake Bay, and up to Baltimore and other big ports.

During the heyday of the Underground Railroad those waterways came to serve as something of an information superhighway as well, with a far-flung network of black dockworkers and sailors surreptitiously spreading news among would-be runaways and their conductors and station masters.

STORY
Flight from the Auction Block

Born a slave sometime around 1815, John Bowley had family roots in the countryside outside of Cambridge, along Harrisville Road and very near the likely site of a long-gone cabin where Harriet Tubman was born. Their families almost certainly knew each other back in that area, which is known as Peter's Neck.

John's owner was a man named Levin Stewart, who belonged to a powerful, prosperous family whose fortunes centered on the sprawling shipbuilding facilities then operating in Madison, a few miles below Cambridge off of the Little Choptank River.

While John was still a little boy, Stewart decided to free his slaves through a legal process known as manumission. This generally involved filing court papers that set specific dates and ages off in the future for when this slave or that one would become legally free.

Stewart filed his papers on a July day in 1817 at the Dorchester County Courthouse, located then and now on High Street, just a few blocks up from the Choptank River Lighthouse. (The building that stood there on the day Stewart filed his papers was destroyed in a later fire; the current courthouse building dates to 1854.)

Manumission was not standard practice among slave owners in those years, but neither was it all that unusual. Some owners freed slaves out of a moral sense that human bondage was wrong, something encouraged by several Methodist preachers in the area. Others used manumission for more selfish reasons, saving themselves the expense and trouble of caring for slaves who were too old or ill to work.

It seems likely that Levin Stewart acted out of good intentions. He had a lot of options, after all. He could have made good money selling his slaves on the open market. Or he could have turned them over, still in bondage, to other members of his family.

Instead, he freed them, one and all, over time. John Bowley became a free man at about the age of 30. By the standards of slavery times, he had enjoyed a rather privileged upbringing up to that point. He entered freedom well equipped with an array of skills that were valuable in the local economy—sailing, shipbuilding, and blacksmithing among them.

Despite his newfound legal status, however, John was not completely free and clear from the bonds of slavery. His wife, Kessiah, remained a slave. Mixed marriages like this were not uncommon, but they were complicated. Slavery was a matrilineal affair, so any children that John and Kessiah had would belong by law to Kessiah's owner.

This is what brought John back to the very same courthouse where Levin Stewart had filed the manumission papers that made John a free man. He was 34 years old on the December day in 1850 when his wife and two young children, James and Araminta, were slated to go up on the auction block outside the courthouse.

Here, too, John was luckier than most of his fellow slaves. Kessiah just so happened to be the niece of Harriet Tubman—in fact, the two women were so close in age that they regarded each other almost as sisters. It's possible that Kessiah and John named their daughter in honor of Tubman, whose name at birth and through her younger years was also Araminta.

Aunt Harriet had escaped slavery the year before, in 1849, and she had decided from the moment she crossed into freedom that she wanted to help her loved ones find their way out of bondage as well. In fact, this would be the very first time Tubman tried to arrange an escape. She was most likely living in either Philadelphia or Cape May, New Jersey at the time, and she presumably received word by way of that surreptitious information highway in the maritime world that Kessiah was headed to the auction block.

Somehow, she and John managed to trade messages and work up the outline of a last-minute plan. Tubman did not come back to Cambridge on this mission.

Instead, she made her way to Baltimore and left John in charge of running the scam they had cooked up.

When Kessiah and the children went up on the block that day, John was the one who placed the winning bid. This was not necessarily something that would have raised suspicion among the local whites. Some free blacks in those days managed to save enough money to buy loved ones out of slavery.

The problem was, John didn't have the money to back up his bid. What happened next is like something out of the Hollywood movie, "The Usual Suspects." The auctioneer closed the bidding and confirmed that John was the winner. Then that auctioneer announced that he was taking a lunch break.

That break was a very convenient turn of events for John Bowley, one that has always left me wondering: Did someone slip that auctioneer a bribe? Is there any chance in the world that the auctioneer was sympathetic to the plight of the Bowleys and did them a favor? Such questions are impossible to answer.

What we can say is that people started walking away once the auctioneer left for lunch. John, Kessiah, and the children joined the exodus. Somehow, they managed to melt into the crowd and fade away altogether.

When the auctioneer returned from lunch, he called for payment on John's winning bid for Kessiah and the children. No one stepped up. Later in life, Tubman and the Bowleys would say only that Kessiah, John, and the children were at that point hiding in a house within five minutes of the courthouse.

We don't know how long they stayed in hiding. It could have been a few hours. It could have been a couple of days. It might have been longer than that.

When the Bowleys emerged from their hideaway, they made their way to a sailboat—there is no telling whose boat it was, or how they came to commandeer it. December is a risky time, weather-wise, to sail from Cambridge to Baltimore, but John was an experienced mariner. Once they got to Baltimore, Aunt Harriet was there to lead John, Kessiah, and the children up through Philadelphia and on to freedom in Canada.

TESTIMONY
Workings of the Grapevine

Booker T. Washington won renown in the late 1800s as an educator, author, and advocate for black-owned businesses. Born in Virginia in 1856, he spent the first few years of his life in slavery. Later, as an adult, he recalled how slaves kept each other abreast of important news during the Civil War.

He is talking here about the workings of an informational grapevine inside of a single plantation, but it's easy to imagine the same sort of network in place across a bigger area, even one as big as the shipyards and ports of the Chesapeake Bay.

Often the slaves got knowledge of the results of great battles before the white people received it.

This news was usually gotten from the coloured man who was sent to the post office for the mail... The man who was sent to the post office would linger about the place long enough to get the drift of the conversation from the group of white people who naturally congregated there, after receiving their mail, to discuss the latest news.

The mail carrier on his way back to our master's house would as naturally retell the news that he had secured among the slaves, and in this way they often heard of important events before the white people at the "big house," as the master's house was called.

POSTSCRIPT
More Heroics from John Bowley

John Bowley's call to duty along the Underground Railroad did not end with freedom for his family. It didn't even end with the freedom of slaves all over the country at the end of the Civil War.

He and Kessiah eventually had seven children. The couple returned home to Dorchester County after the Civil War with most of those children in tow, settling in the black community that was then centered along Old Field Road in the Church Creek area.

There, John and Kessiah learned that blacks still faced all manner of discrimination and oppression, even after emancipation. Slave owners could be quite a crafty lot, and some of them played fast and loose with the rules of indenture and apprenticeship, basically transforming those legal arrangements into a new kind of slavery.

One of Harriet Tubman's brothers had two sons caught up in this kind of predicament. And so twice in the latter part of the 1860s, John Bowley sailed across the Choptank River over to Trappe, in Talbot County. He rescued first one and then another of those boys, and then he and Kessiah helped them make their way up to Auburn, New York, where they were reunited with their father after many years apart.

Kessiah passed away in 1897. She was in her early 70s. Her will made John a beneficiary of her estate, so he must have lived on after her. No one seems to have located a record of his death yet.

CONNECTIONS

- The story of Harriet Tubman's early years in Peter's Neck—the same area where John Bowley was born— is in Chapter 4.
- The two young men that John Bowley rescued from Talbot County in the late 1860s were the sons of Tubman's brother Robert Ross, who adopted the name John Stewart in freedom. The story of Robert's flight from bondage with two other brothers is told in three parts in Chapter 5, Chapter 7, and Chapter 14.

TRAVEL RESOURCES

The **Dorchester County Courthouse** is located at 206 High Street in Cambridge, Maryland. There is an interpretive sign about the Underground Railroad outside the building, along with a kiosk offering brochures and travel information.

The courthouse is right in downtown Cambridge, where there are a good number of shops, restaurants, and attractions. Information about things to do and places to go in and around Cambridge is available from **Dorchester County Tourism**.

- The Dorchester Visitor Center is at 2 Rose Hill Place, Cambridge, Maryland
- VisitDorchester.org; Facebook.com/DorchesterCounty; 410.228.1000

The **Harriet Tubman Underground Railroad Byway** runs through both Dorchester and Caroline counties in Maryland and then on into Delaware.

- Maryland: HarrietTubmanByway.org; Facebook.com/HarrietTubmanByway; 410.228.1000
- Delaware: TubmanBywayDelaware.org

3: SIDE TRIP: THE HARRIET TUBMAN MUSEUM AND EDUCATIONAL CENTER

Cambridge, Maryland

Lots of organizations regard themselves as grassroots affairs, but few embody the term quite so well as the Harriet Tubman Organization, which operates a little storefront museum in the heart of downtown Cambridge, Maryland.

The old saying that fame is fleeting certainly applies in the case of Harriet Tubman over the big arc of time. Tubman did her heroic work in obscurity, winning admiration in her younger years only among a small circle of hard-core Underground Railroad activists. She did win a good measure of national renown later in her life, after the Civil War and during the women's suffrage movement.

By the middle years of the 20th century, however, she had fallen back into obscurity. If you had come to Cambridge curious about Harriet Tubman in the 1970s, you wouldn't have found any sites to see or historical markers to read. The only option available back then involved somehow finding your way to the home of Addie Clash Travers. "Miss Addie" served for several decades as the repository of all local lore related to the "Moses of Her People."

Travers joined forces back then with a little group of locals that launched an annual Harriet Ross Tubman Day celebration at the history-laden Bazzel's Methodist Episcopal Church in Tubman's old childhood stomping grounds of Bucktown. That event spurred the formation of a more formal group, the Harriet Tubman Association of Dorchester County, which had its headquarters in the private home of Russell and Rev. Blanch Bailey on Pine Street in Cambridge.

The Harriet Tubman Organization took on its current form in the early 1980s. By the time I arrived in Cambridge in the mid-2000s, its leadership was in the hands of Evelyn Townsend, an elegant retired schoolteacher in her 80s. The notion of Harriet Tubman as an important figure in American history and a driver for local tourism was just starting to pick up steam. As of this writing, a local plumber named Donald Pinder is the group's leader.

The Tubman organization remains quite true to its grassroots history. The little museum, staffed entirely by community volunteers, is definitely worth a visit. The exhibit panels are modest, but well done. Plus, it's an opportunity for visitors to meet and chat with the modern-day locals who are still doing their part to stay true to the vision "Miss Addie" had way back when, that the community where Harriet Tubman was born should treat her legacy as a treasure of the highest order.

TRAVEL RESOURCES

It's best to call ahead before visiting the **Harriet Tubman Museum and Educational Center** to make sure that a volunteer will be on hand for your visit. Guided group tours of Tubman sites in the area are also available through the center.

- 424 Race Street, Cambridge, Maryland
- 410.228.0401

Three other sites in Cambridge feature Tubman materials that may be of interest. Several Tubman-related exhibit panels are part of the larger display about local history at the **Dorchester County Visitor Center**.

- 2 Rose Hill Place, Cambridge, Maryland
- VisitDorchester.org; Facebook.com/DorchesterCounty; 410.228.1000

Tubman is prominently featured in a mural by nationally known artist Michael Rosato that celebrates the African-American history of Dorchester County. That mural is on a building at the intersection of **U.S. Route 50 and Maryland Avenue**, which is quite near the Visitor Center above.

The **Harriet Tubman Memorial Garden** is tucked away in a patch of greenery at the bend along Route 50 as it makes its way through Cambridge. The murals here were painted by a local member of Tubman's family, Charles Ross.

- Washington Street at Route 50, Cambridge, Maryland (The easiest address to use for directions is that of the Cambridge Public Safety Building, 8 Washington Street—the garden is right across the street.)
- HarrietTubmanByway.org/harriet-tubman-memorial-garden/

4: Welcome to the World, Araminta

Dorchester County, Maryland

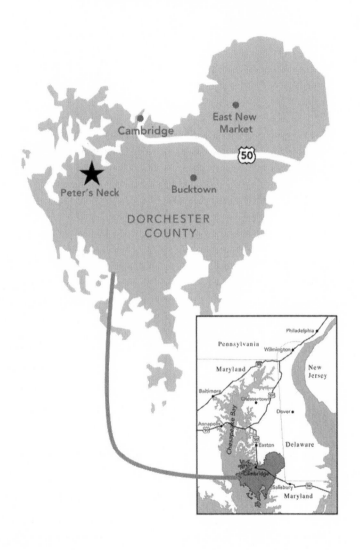

BIG PICTURE
The Harriet Tubman Discussion Group

Shortly after moving to Cambridge, Maryland in the mid-2000s I became a regular at the monthly meetings of the Harriet Tubman Discussion Group. Held in the local library, these affairs had a rag-tag aspect. The group's leader, John Creighton, would show up in work pants and a baseball hat, carting a dog-eared cardboard box full of photocopied documents, from old Sanborn fire insurance maps to estate inventories, census documents, newspaper clippings, and more.

He and his partner, Pat Lewis, would then proceed to make our heads spin by dancing their way through those documents in rat-a-tat-tat fashion, connecting a myriad of little dots from this source and that one and this other one, too, until they formed a coherent picture of what probably happened during this, that, or another episode in Tubman's life.

John had been at this work for a long time before I started showing up. A onetime schoolteacher and self-taught historian, he devoted the last half of his life to Tubman research, embracing that undertaking long before his subject became fashionable.

Today, of course, the situation is different. Lots of experts have been digging into the Tubman story in recent years, and they have managed to unearth some important new findings and turn out some interesting new biographies. I suspect, however, that most, if not all, of those experts would readily concede that their accomplishments were built in part on a foundation that John Creighton laid down over the years in his vast collection of old-school, hand-scrawled index cards.

One Discussion Group Saturday, John decided to lead an impromptu field trip out to the place where Harriet Tubman was most likely born. Four or five of us went along, caravan-style, making our way out of town and then through Church Creek along Route 16 before turning onto Harrisville Road. We kept on past the point where the pavement ends, following the dirt road that continues from there through a patch of privately owned forestlands.

No remnant of Tubman or her times awaits at the end of Harrisville Road. There is nothing specific to see or do once you get there. No one knows the location of the cabin hereabouts where she likely came into the world.

John was uncharacteristically quiet that afternoon. He stood amid those trees in silent thought, presumably imagining what this neck of the woods looked like in the early 1820s and how the events of those days might have played out in the life of one family in particular as it welcomed a new baby girl into the world.

John had a reverent look on his face in that moment, like someone in the midst of a religious pilgrimage. That's the look I remember whenever he pops into my mind nowadays. John passed away a couple of years back. He is buried right here in Peter's Neck, in the graveyard of the historic Malone's Church on nearby White Marsh Road. May he rest in peace.

STORY
Welcome to the World, Araminta

Traveling along Route 16 out near Madison, your eyes will most likely gravitate to the north side of the road. There, the view serves up a series of now-you-see-it-now-you-don't glimpses of the Little Choptank River and its tributaries.

This story, however, is set to the south, where it's mostly farm fields and stands of trees. The backroads that head off into this landscape are little-used affairs, with a small gaggle of houses clustered together up near the main road petering out quickly into the occasional hunting cabin or trailer home.

The scenery has a timeless aspect, but don't let that fool you. The landscape here has been through a world of change over the centuries. In the early 1800s, for example, this was the epicenter of the region's timber industry. The nearby Madison waterfront was a bustling shipbuilding center during the timber rush years.

The land known as Peter's Neck lies between Harrisville and White Marsh roads. It was filled with black families back then—some free, some enslaved, just about all engaged in one fashion or another in the work of clearing timber and getting it to market.

One landowner here, Anthony Thompson, decided to build an overland path to make it easier to transport timber and supplies. The road that we know today as Harrisville was originally called Thompson's New Road.

Thompson had about 40 slaves working on this land, including a first-rate timbering supervisor named Ben Ross. Thompson also managed a handful of slaves that belonged to his stepson, Edward Brodess, who was still a minor.

This is the way Ben Ross came to meet and marry one of the Brodess slaves, Rit Green. They would eventually have nine children together. By the start of 1822, four had been born and the fifth was on the way. The oldest Ross child, Linah, was about 14 at this point. The youngest, Robert, was six or seven. In between were two more girls, Mariah Ritty and Soph.

The landscape where these children grew up was nothing like the sparsely traveled areas you will see out that way these days. Both Harrisville and White Marsh roads would have been filled with the dust and noise of wagons and horses and foot traffic. They would have been lined with cabins, each of which had its own yard full of scampering chickens, hanging laundry, roaring fires, and children running this way and that.

When that fifth child arrived in February, Ben and Rit named her Araminta. Everyone called her "Minty." She was born into a family that had enjoyed a long, 15-or-so-year run of togetherness in the same area and perhaps even the same cabin.

Alas, that stability would soon come to an end and give way to an equally long stretch marked by separation, loss, grief, and anger in the Ross family. Minty was about two years old when her owner, Edward Brodess, turned 21 and moved out of the Thompson household and into his own place, 10 miles away in the village of Bucktown. He took his slaves with him, which meant separating Rit and the children from her husband and their father.

Minty was just three when Brodess sold one of her sisters, Mariah Ritty, to a slave trader from the Deep South. No one in the family would ever see or hear from Mariah again.

The worst was yet to come. In the 1830s, Brodess sold two other sisters, Soph and Linah. Both were young mothers by this point in their lives, and both were torn away from their children. Soph and Linah, too, would never be seen or heard from again.

Later in life, in an interview with a reporter, Tubman's older brother, Robert, recalled his memories of the day Linah disappeared. He had landed in a strange spot of trouble that could happen only in slavery times, having been jailed in connection with debts owed not by himself, but by his owner. He was sitting in a cell when his sister was brought in.

[She had been] taken away from her children, handcuffed, and put into the jail where I was. Her irons were taken off; she was in great grief, crying all the time. "Oh my children! My poor children!"

47

til it appeared to me, she would kill herself for grief.

Sarah Bradford published the first biography of Tubman in 1869. Her work on that and another, later biography was based on a series of in-person sessions with her subject. This is how she describes what Harriet went through when Linah and Soph were sold away:

> [Her] two older sisters [had been] taken away as part of a chain gang, and they had gone no one knew whither; she had seen the agonized expression on their faces as they turned to take a last look at their "Old Cabin Home;" and had watched them from the top of the fence, as they went off weeping and lamenting, till they were hidden from her sight forever.

In her book, *Harriet Tubman: Imagining a Life*, the writer Beverly Lowry plays an interesting guessing game about how these events might have affected Minty as she made it through childhood and grew up to become Harriet Tubman. Did all that fracturing of her family in those early years turn Harriet into the "fix-it child," who would remain bound and determined for all the rest of her days to try and put her Humpty-Dumpty of a family back together again?

TESTIMONY
'You Couldn't Guess de Awfulness of It'

Former slave Delia Garlic was interviewed at the age of 100 by a writer working with the Federal Writers' Project during the Depression years. The session took place in Montgomery, Alabama, and appears in *When I Was a Slave: Memoirs from the Slave Narrative Collection.*

I was born at Powhatan, Virginia, and was the youngest of thirteen chillen. I never seed none of my brothers and sisters 'cept brother William.

Him and my mother and me was brought in a speculator's drove to Richmond and put in a warehouse with a drove of other niggers. Den we was all put on a block and sold to de highest bidder.

I never seed brother William again. Mammy and me was sold to a man by the name of Carter, who was de sheriff of de county. Dey wasn't no good times at his house.

It's bad to belong to folks dat own you soul and body, dat can tie you up to a tree, with yo' face to d' tree and yo' arms fastened tight around it, who take a long curlin' whip and cut de blood every lick. Folks a mile away could hear dem awful whippings. Dey was a terrible part of livin'.

Slavery days was hell. I was growed up when de War come, and I was a mother before it closed.

Babies was snatched from dere mother's breast and sold to speculators. Chillens was separated from sisters and brothers and never saw each other again.

'Course dey cry. You think they not cry when dey was sold like cattle? I could tell you about it all day, but even den you couldn't guess de awfulness of it.

CONNECTIONS

- The Kessiah Bowley who escaped from the auction block at the Dorchester County Courthouse in 1850 was the daughter of Linah Ross, Harriet Tubman's sister. Kessiah's husband, John Bowley, grew up in the Peter's Neck area. Their story is in Chapter 2.
- The free black farmer Jacob Jackson lived just a little way up the road from Peter's Neck. The story of how he and Tubman worked together during the famed "Christmas Escape" of 1854 is in Chapter 5.
- Harriet Tubman would spend a good deal of time back in the Peter's Neck area as a young woman. That story is in Chapter 6.

TRAVEL RESOURCES

There is not much in the way of visitor amenities out this way. You will pass the **Woolford General Store**, 1614 Taylors Island Road in Woolford, Maryland, just before coming to Harrisville Road. It offers essentials and sandwiches in a down-home atmosphere.

Parts of the Peter's Neck area are popular with hunters. Please respect the no trespassing signs and remember to bring along some blaze orange to wear in season.

Information about things to do and places to go in and around Dorchester County is available from **Dorchester County Tourism**.

- The Dorchester Visitor Center is at 2 Rose Hill Place, Cambridge, Maryland
- VisitDorchester.org; Facebook.com/DorchesterCounty; 410.228.1000

The **Harriet Tubman Underground Railroad Byway** runs through both Dorchester and Caroline counties in Maryland and then on into Delaware.

- Maryland: HarrietTubmanByway.org; Facebook.com/HarrietTubmanByway; 410.228.1000
- Delaware: TubmanBywayDelaware.org

5: 'The Good Old Ship of Zion' (Christmas Escape, Part 1)

Dorchester County, Maryland

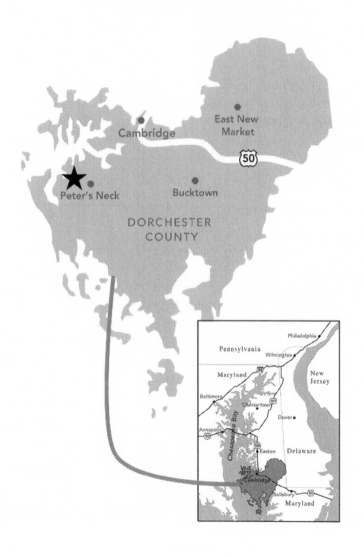

BIG PICTURE
The Thin Line

Along the Underground Railroad the line that separated *brave* from *reckless* could be quite thin. Harriet Tubman is often celebrated for her bravery—and rightly so. That's a trait she exhibited every time she came back down into Maryland to lead her family and friends to freedom.

She was usually quite cautious in the way she went about that work. She had a keen sense for the presence of danger. At the slightest sign of trouble, she would send passengers into hiding, sometimes for days at a stretch.

She had an array of tricks up her sleeve to help avoid detection. Even as a young woman in her 30s, she was quite adept at disguising herself as a frail old lady. She would also feign ignorance and stupidity, playing into the preconceptions white people had about black women.

There was an occasion in 1854, however, when it seems to me that Tubman threw caution to the wind and crossed the line into *reckless* territory. At the center of that story is Jacob Jackson, a free black man who lived along Route 16 just beyond the Peter's Neck area where we left off in the last chapter.

Here is the question that I would pose to help you start thinking about the story that follows: What precious thing in your life would drive you to throw caution to the wind? I am not talking here about breaking the speed limit because you're late for a meeting, or running your credit card balance up too high around the holidays. I'm talking about the sort of recklessness that puts the freedom of a trusted friend at risk, so much so that he might lose everything and land in jail.

STORY
'The Good Old Ship of Zion'

Jacob Jackson must have been quite the prominent member of his community. Not many free blacks on the Eastern Shore managed to run their own 40-acre farms in slavery times. Not many knew how to read, either. This latter skill is what Harriet Tubman would try and make use of in one of her most famous operations, the Christmas Escape of 1854.

Not much else is known about Jackson, though that could change in the coming years. His old home site along Route 16, between White Marsh Road and Woolford Creek, is now owned by the National Park Service. Officials there have talked in a preliminary way about grand plans to locate old foundations, erect replica buildings, and open the site to the public, but any such developments are still many years off as of this writing in 2017.

It's impossible to say how well Tubman and Jackson knew each other. The site of Tubman's birth is quite close to that of Jackson's farm. She lived and worked in this same area for a lengthy stretch of her teens and

20s. Her father was a prominent figure hereabouts as well, managing the timbering operations of a major landowner in the area.

It's impossible, too, to say how connected Jackson might have been with the larger Underground Railroad. The fact that Tubman called on him in a moment of crisis indicates that she knew Jackson could be trusted, but no evidence has surfaced yet that he ever harbored fugitives on his farm or served as a conductor or station master.

The precious thing that drove Tubman to put the freedom of her friend Jacob Jackson at risk was her family. By late 1854, five years had passed since Tubman's own flight to freedom. Most of her family belonged at this point to Eliza Brodess, the widow of their former owner, Edward Brodess.

Historians who have looked over household ledgers from this period say that Eliza was engaged in the 19th century equivalent of running up a credit card. There were too many purchases of fancy clothes and fashionable baubles and not enough in the way of mundane farm supplies. Eliza decided that the solution to her financial woes involved selling three slaves. Ben, Henry, and Robert Ross—Tubman's brothers—were scheduled to go up on the auction block in Cambridge on December 26.

When Tubman received this news along the Underground Railroad grapevine, it must have struck her to the core. As a child, she had lost three older sisters to slave traders from the Deep South. Now, three brothers faced the same fate.

The Woolford post office stands today along Route 16 on the way out to the Jackson site. I am not sure where such a facility operated back in Tubman's day, but I do know that the mail service worked a little differently then. Most every piece of mail sent to most every black person in this area got opened and inspected by white people before getting delivered. Those white people were always on the lookout for clues about runaway slaves and who might be helping them out.

Tubman herself did not know how to read or write, so she would recite her letters while others handled the actual penmanship. The letter she prepared for Jackson was signed in the name of his adoptive son, William Henry Jackson. There was some small talk in it at the beginning, and then there was this:

> Read my letter to the old folks, and give my love to them, and tell my brothers to be always watching unto prayer, and when the good old ship of Zion comes along, to be ready to step on board.

The white men inspecting Jackson's mail didn't know what to make of this passage. They knew that William Henry was a free black man living in Canada. But they also knew that he didn't have any brothers. They took the letter to Jackson and demanded an explanation. Here is what he said:

"Dat letter can't be meant for me no how. I can't make head or tail of it."

This apparently left the inspectors in a state of confusion, and they seem to have decided to just leave the matter alone. After the interrogation, Jackson set about alerting the three Ross brothers that their sister was coming for them. We will get to what happened next on the journey those brothers took to freedom in Chapter 7.

But the question this chapter leaves in my mind is this: *What if?* What if one of those inspectors had been a bit smarter or a bit more cautious? Tubman's coded message was clever enough, as far as it goes, but it wasn't exactly as foolproof as a modern-day encrypted computer file.

She must have known how much danger she was putting her friend in by sending this letter. The consequences for Jackson ran beyond arrest and imprisonment—there were cases from this period in which free blacks were sold into slavery for life after being caught helping runaways. And so I wonder: Just how big was the sigh of relief that Tubman let loose upon learning that Jackson had emerged from this affair unscathed?

TESTIMONY
Spiritual Connections

This is the first time in our Underground Railroad travels that the topic of old spirituals, such as the "Old Ship of Zion," has arisen, but it won't be the last. Tubman used these songs to send coded messages on several other occasions as well.

It's hard to tell looking back through the mists of history which version of "Old Ship of Zion" might have been most familiar to Tubman and Jacob Jackson, but this version of the lyrics should give a pretty good sense for the power and promise the song must have held for people living their lives in bondage and hearing rumors about the freedom that awaited somewhere off in the North.

'Tis the old ship of Zion,
'Tis the old ship of Zion,
'Tis the old ship of Zion,
Get on board, get on board.

She has angels for the sailors, (thrice)
Get on board, get on board.

That ship is out-a sailing, sailing, sailing, (thrice)
Get on board, get on board.

She's a-sailing mighty steady, steady, steady, (thrice)

Get on board, get on board.

There's no danger on that water, (thrice)
Get on board, get on board.

She has landed many-a thousand, (thrice)
Get on board, get on board.

King Jesus is the captain, captain, captain,
(thrice)
Get on board, get on board.

'Tis the old ship of Zion,
'Tis the old ship of Zion,
'Tis the old ship of Zion,
And she's making for the Promised Land.

CONNECTIONS

- I have split the Christmas Escape into three chapters. The second is in Chapter 7. The third is in Chapter 14.

TRAVEL RESOURCES

As of this writing in 2017, the Jacob Jackson site is unmarked and closed to visitors. There are no buildings or other elements on the landscape that survive from slavery days. The site stands along Taylors Island Road between White Marsh Road and Woolford Creek.

There is not much in the way of visitor amenities out this way. The **Woolford General Store**—1614 Taylors Island Road in Woolford, Maryland—offers essentials and sandwiches in a down-home atmosphere. In Madison, there is a little restaurant— **Millie's at Madison**, 4814 Madison Canning House Road—that overlooks the marina in a pretty little spot called Caper's Wharf.

Information about things to do and places to go in and around Dorchester County is available from **Dorchester County Tourism**.
- Dorchester Visitor Center, 2 Rose Hill Place, Cambridge, Maryland
- VisitDorchester.org; Facebook.com/DorchesterCounty; 410.228.1000

The **Harriet Tubman Underground Railroad Byway** runs through both Dorchester and Caroline counties in Maryland and then on into Delaware.
- Maryland: HarrietTubmanByway.org; Facebook.com/HarrietTubmanByway; 410.228.1000
- Delaware: TubmanBywayDelaware.org

6: 'I PRAYED ALL DE TIME'
(HARRIET'S ESCAPE, PART 1)

Dorchester County, Maryland

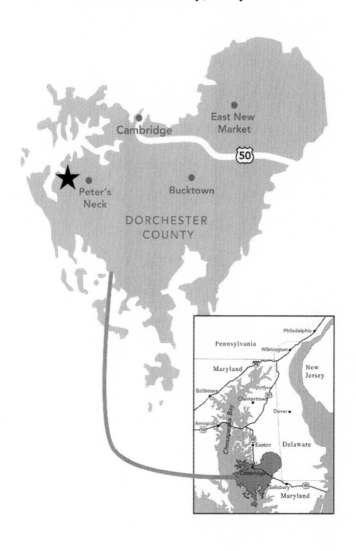

BIG PICTURE
Minty Comes of Age

During her teen years, Harriet Tubman was still known by her given name, Araminta Ross. Everyone called her "Minty." There is a lot we don't know about her journey through adolescence, but there are a few big-picture bits and pieces that point to the possibility that she might have had a rough go of it.

Minty entered those teen years as a tiny, fragile, and unhealthy thing. She was still recovering from the after-effects of a near-fatal blow to the head that she had suffered at a crossroads store in Bucktown, Maryland, where she had refused to help a white man trying to catch a young black boy fleeing from the prospect of punishment. That white man flung a two-pound metal weight across the store. He was aiming for the boy, but he struck Minty instead.

Were teenagers different in the 1830s than they are today? Did kids back then, too, obsess over the way their peers saw them?

The aftereffects of Minty's injuries must have left her feeling like an oddball. It wasn't just that she was sickly and weak. She also suffered from bouts of a strange sleeping sickness that made her nod off in the blink of an eye at unusual and unpredictable moments. She had most likely started seeing half-crazy visions in her mind by this point, too. She might even have started to wonder whether those visions were messages from God.

Did the other kids make fun of her for being weak and weird? How badly did Minty wish she could just be a "normal" kid and fit in?

We all know how the Harriet Tubman story turns out. We know that she would come through this adolescence just fine and go on to become an American hero for the ages. But Minty herself had no way of knowing that in the mid-1830s. Back then, she was just another strange young girl on the brink of womanhood, and I imagine that she endured her share of confusion and self-doubt on her journey through adolescence.

STORY
'I Prayed All de Time'

Edward Brodess didn't think much of the future prospects of his young slave, Minty, in the wake of the injuries she suffered at the Bucktown store. He tried to sell her in this period, but who would pay good money for a slave girl who might be an invalid for a long time to come?

Brodess did find a way to get something out of his property eventually. In 1836, he hired Minty out to a man named John T. Stewart, which involved her moving out of Bucktown and back to the area around Peter's Neck, where she had been born and where her father, Ben Ross, still lived. She would work for Stewart for the next six years.

The tasks she tackled in this period were as hard and physical as they come, but something about pitching in with crews that chopped down tall trees, transported huge bundles of logs, and drove wagons powered by teams of unruly oxen seems to have been a powerful tonic for her fragile health. Later in life, she would speak with great pride about how she was able to hold her own in this male-dominated world.

The best place along Route 16 to stop and think about the years when Minty came of age is south of Madison, on the way to Taylors Island. There is a little bridge out there where the road crosses over a thin spit of water. The roadside sign there says, "Parsons Creek." The shoulder here is wide enough to pull off to the side so that you can get out and give it a look.

The first thing you will see is that it's drop-dead gorgeous out here. The marshlands and woods to the south are all part of Blackwater National Wildlife Refuge. The widening water on the other side of the road is heading off into the Little Choptank River, which, as you will see off in the distance, isn't so "little" at all.

The sign identifying this as Parsons Creek is misleading, at least for our Tubman-travel purposes. This isn't a "creek" at all. And it wasn't called "Parsons" back in slavery times. This was Stewart's Canal then.

The fact that it runs straight as an arrow is a sure giveaway to its unnatural origins. Mother Nature never goes about her work in the sort of straight line you see when looking up Stewart's Canal, which was dug out over the course of decades by the human hands of slaves and free blacks. Its purpose was to facilitate the transport of logs out of Stewart-family-owned forestlands and into the shipyard in Madison.

There is no telling for sure whether Minty or her father worked directly along the canal, perhaps transporting timber to its shores or along its waters. But the view from the little bridge will nonetheless fuel your imagination when it comes to the back-breaking nature of the work of the timbering industry back then. Can you even imagine how bad the biting flies and monstrous mosquitoes were out there in the warmer months?

Anthony Thompson, the owner of Ben Ross, died in 1836. His will stipulated that Ben would become a free man in five years' time. It also said he would be given a plot of his own on Thompson family land, where he could build a cabin and live out the rest of his years. This is how Ben and Rit Ross came to move 25 or so miles up to Poplar Neck, on the Choptank River in Caroline County. Thompson's son, Anthony C. Thompson, owned a lot of timberland up that way.

Somewhere in this period, Minty Ross met John Tubman. By the time they got to courting, that weak, sickly girl had come out on the other side of her adolescence as an uncommonly strong woman. Minty was 22 or 23 when she and John got married in about 1844. By the standards of slavery times, that was rather late in life to be tying the knot.

The marriage inspired Minty to change not just her last name, but her first as well. From here on out she would be Harriet Tubman. Presumably, that new first name was a tribute to her mother.

As for John Tubman, he is mostly a mystery. Beyond his status as a free black man, we know little about him. It's impossible to track where, precisely, the couple lived during all of the years in this period, but we do know that Harriet's owner hired her out to Anthony C. Thompson between 1847 and 1849, so she was almost certainly living with or near her parents at Poplar Neck in that window.

Harriet still had that sleeping sickness. In fact, the visions that came into her mind took a frightening turn in the early years of her marriage. In one such recurring dream, a team of riders atop galloping horses would swoop into view and fill Harriet's head with terrifying sounds—the clamor of clattering hooves and the cries of mothers whose children were being yanked from their arms.

In another, Harriet had the gift of flight. She would be soaring high above fields and towns, "like a bird," but then reach a point where a strange barrier appeared, something along the lines of an invisible fence or an airborne river. In one variation, this dream had a happy ending.

It 'peared like I wouldn't have the strength, and just as I was sinkin' down, there would be ladies all drest in white over there, and they would put out their arms and pull me 'cross.

In other variations, however, this dream took a frightful turn.

> [B]eautiful white ladies ... stretched out their arms to me over the line, but I couldn't reach them nohow, [and] I always fell before I got to the line.

Her husband dismissed these dreams. In later years Harriet would recall how John compared his wife to a character from folklore known as "old Cudjo." Cudjo never understood that something was a joke until long after everyone else was done laughing about it. But Harriet took her visions seriously. She was more convinced than ever that they were messages from God.

Early in 1849, Harriet began hearing rumors that her owner, Edward Brodess, was about to sell off some slaves. Later in life, Harriet would tell her biographer, Sarah Bradford, that she even endured inspections by slave dealers during this period.

As a young girl, Harriet had been through the heartbreak of losing three older sisters at the auction block. Now here she was, possibly heading toward that fate herself. The stress of the situation got to her. Or perhaps she simply caught some bug. In any case, Harriet fell ill and spent a long stretch of time confined to her bed.

> And so as I lay so sick ... from Christmas till March, I was always praying for poor ole master.

'Pears like I didn't do nothing but pray for ole master.

"Oh, Lord, convert ole master."

"Oh, dear Lord, change dat man's heart, and make him a Christian."

And all the time he was bringing men to look at me, and dey stood there saying what dey would give, and what dey would take, and all I could say was, "Oh, Lord, convert ole master."

Den I heard dat as soon as I was able to move I was to be sent with my brudders, in the chain-gang to de far South. Then I changed my prayer, and I said,

"Lord, if you ain't never going to change dat man's heart, kill him, Lord, and take him out of de way, so he won't do no more mischief."

Next ting I heard ole master was dead; and he died just as he had lived, a wicked, bad man.

Oh, den it 'peared like I would give de world full of silver and gold, if I had it, to bring dat pore soul back, I would give myself; I would give eberyting! But he was gone, I couldn't pray for him no more.

Brodess died in March of 1849. Harriet's worries that it was the power of her prayers that had caused his death sent her into a frenzy of pleading with God for forgiveness.

'Pears like, I prayed all de time.... I was always talking to de Lord. When I went to the horse-trough to wash my face, and took up de water in my hands, I said, "Oh, Lord, wash me, make me clean." When I took up de towel to wipe my face and hands, I cried, "Oh, Lord, for Jesus' sake, wipe away all my sins!" When I took up de broom and began to sweep, I groaned, "Oh, Lord, whatsoebber sin dere be in my heart, sweep it out, Lord, clar and clean;" but I can't pray no more for pore ole master.

The death of an owner often left his or her slaves in a state of great uncertainty. Who would their new owner be? Would they be sold away to pay off estate debts? Minty's dreams grew even more intense. Those violent men atop those galloping horses swept through her head over and over again.

Oh, dey're comin', dey're comin' I mus' go!

Then it began. The first notice that some Brodess slaves were going up on the block involved a 20-year-old woman named Harriet and her 2-year-old daughter. It's possible that this was a niece of Tubman's named Harriet Jolley. The sale of this other Harriet landed on the back burner after getting caught up in legal complications with the estate. Then another notice went up, this time announcing the coming sale of Kessiah Bowley. This was definitely one of Tubman's nieces. The sale of Kessiah ended up getting delayed by those legal complications, too.

How long would the delays last? Whose name would show up in the next notice of a pending sale? The thought that took hold in Tubman's head and heart during these frightful days involved a bold and drastic step.

I had reasoned dis out in my mind; there was one of two things I had a *right* to, liberty, or death; if I could not have one, I would have de oder.

POSTSCRIPT
'If He Could Do Without Her, She Could Do Without Him'

The marriage of John and Harriet Tubman did not end happily. Two years after she herself escaped in 1849, Harriet returned to Dorchester County in hopes of reuniting with John and getting him to join her in the North.

What she found instead was that John had given up on their marriage and was living with another woman. Harriet's instinctive response to this news was a surge of rage. The writer Ednah Cheney recalled Tubman saying that in this moment she wanted to march "right in and make all the trouble" she could over John's betrayal. She forced herself to calm down instead, thinking about "how foolish it was just for temper to make mischief."

In the end, she decided that if he could do without her, well, she could do without him.

There is one more turn to this story, and it's a tragic one that dates to later years, after the Civil War. One morning in October 1867, John Tubman got into some sort of an argument with a white man named Robert Vincent. The two eventually went their separate ways but when Vincent saw Tubman on the road later that day, he pulled out a pistol and shot him. Vincent went on trial for the murder in Dorchester County, but he was acquitted.

CONNECTIONS

- I have placed the second part of the story of Harriet's escape at Red Bridges in the Caroline County town of Greensboro, Maryland. It's in Chapter 18.
- Kessiah Bowley, the niece of Harriet Tubman's who very nearly went up for sale here, would end up going up on the block in December 1850. The story of how she was rescued that day is in Chapter 2.
- The land where Ben Ross built his cabin on Poplar Neck, near Preston, was a key spot in Harriet Tubman's life. There are two stories in this book set there, one in Chapter 14 and the other in Chapter 15.

TRAVEL RESOURCES

Stewart's Canal comes up a couple of miles after White Marsh Road on the way to Taylors Island. The most important landmark to look for as you approach is that sign saying "Parsons Creek." If you get to Smithville Road, you've gone too far.

When you pull over on the shoulder here and get out to look at the canal, please be extra careful, especially if you have kids in tow. Cars and trucks will be moving at highway speeds.

Information about things to do and places to go in and around Dorchester County is available from **Dorchester County Tourism**.

- Dorchester Visitor Center, 2 Rose Hill Place, Cambridge, Maryland
- VisitDorchester.org; Facebook.com/DorchesterCounty; 410.228.1000

The **Harriet Tubman Underground Railroad Byway** runs through both Dorchester and Caroline counties in Maryland and then on into Delaware.

- Maryland: HarrietTubmanByway.org; Facebook.com/HarrietTubmanByway; 410.228.1000
- Delaware: TubmanBywayDelaware.org

7: Love Stories at Buttons Creek (Christmas Escape, Part 2)

Dorchester County, Maryland

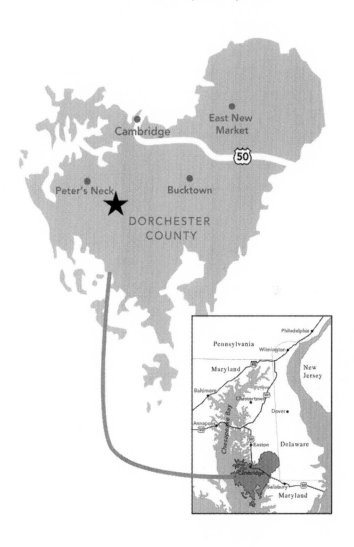

BIG PICTURE
Hopeless in Love

I recommend that you take the long way around to Buttons Creek from the point where we left off in the last chapter at Stewart's Canal (aka Parsons Creek). Keep on Route 16 toward Taylors Island, turning left before the island at Smithville Road, which is a sweet, serene affair that meanders through the marshlands of the Blackwater National Wildlife Refuge. Where the road ends, turn left at Route 335, and then follow that as it makes another left and heads back toward Cambridge through little Golden Hill and a lot more marshland.

You will come in time to a long, low bridge over the Little Blackwater River. Where that bridge ends, there is a roadside pull-off on the left that's a popular launching point with the kayaking and fishing set. Just up that river, to the northwest, is the mouth of little Buttons Creek, one of the prettiest paddling destinations on Maryland's Eastern Shore.

Back in Harriet Tubman's day, there was a farm along Buttons Creek that was home to an enslaved woman named Jane Kane. The twists and turns in the story of her escape from bondage match the meandering course of the creek, which is what makes this a perfect place to stop and think about how complicated matters of love and marriage could get in slavery times.

At the age of 22, Jane was in love with a guy named Ben. He was a slave, too, but he had a different owner and lived on a different farm. Their prospects for a happy life together were pretty dim. Jane belonged to a cruel man named Horatio Jones. He had once beaten her so mercilessly that blood poured as if from a faucet from both her mouth and her nose. On another occasion, he had whipped Jane's brother to the point where his back looked like a side of raw beef.

As Jane's owner, Jones had the power to decide whom she could marry. When it came to Ben, he said no. If he bothered to give Jane a reason for this refusal, it has not been recorded in history books. But a bit of educated guesswork might get us in the neighborhood of the way Jones's mind was working.

Slavery was a matrilineal affair, with legal rights to the ownership of newborn children passing through the mother and having nothing at all to do with the father. Slave owners like Jones often took a keen interest in the love lives of their female slaves during childbearing years. There seems to have been a whole pseudoscience popular with his set about which body types in a father should be matched with which types in a mother so as to generate children who would grow up into the strongest possible laborers and fetch the highest possible price tags.

Jones might also have regarded Ben as a risky character who might sweet talk Jane into running away. Ben had tried to run off once before, after all, though he had returned voluntarily out of fear of getting caught.

There was also the matter of his sister, who had run off without returning. Her name was Harriet Tubman.

I haven't come across any reports that Ben was ever beaten the way Jane and her brother were, but his situation at the end of 1854 was pretty hopeless as well. He was owned by Eliza Brodess, a widow who had inherited Ben and his siblings after the death of her husband five years before. Eliza now found herself mired in financial difficulties, and the solution she devised involved cashing in on Ben and two of his brothers.

In a newspaper ad that December, Brodess announced that Ben, Robert, and Henry Ross would be going up on the slave auction block in Cambridge on the day after Christmas.

STORY
Love Stories at Buttons Creek

That newspaper ad was a terrible blow for Ben's brother Robert, too. He was already married. He and his wife, Mary, had two young sons, John and Moses. A third child was on the way. Few stories along the Underground Railroad are as heart-wrenching as what Robert and Mary endured on the night before Harriet Tubman led her brothers on a run for freedom.

By this point, Harriet Tubman was living in St. Catharine's, Ontario, just across the Canadian border from Buffalo, New York. There is some speculation among historians that she was already at work on plans to rescue her brothers when she received word through the Underground Railroad grapevine that they were about to go up on the auction block. Now there was no time to spare. She arranged for a coded message to be sent in a letter to a free black friend, Jacob Jackson. Jackson then alerted the three Ross brothers that their sister was on the way, and that they should be ready to get on board "the good old ship of Zion."

When Tubman arrived in the area, she sent word along that grapevine about the place and time for a rendezvous. Robert would end up being late to that gathering, but for good reason. His wife, Mary, had gone into labor with their third child. First, he had to find a midwife for her. Then he decided to wait and make sure everything went all right with the delivery. After that, he still had a world of trouble trying to tear himself away from her bedside, and from his new daughter. He and Mary agreed to name that baby Harriet.

All we have from their time together that night is a snippet of conversation recorded years after the fact by Harriet Tubman's biographer, Sarah Bradford. Mary sensed a restlessness in her husband. She grew worried that he was going to run off.

What was in her mind in this moment? Could she have been unaware that Robert was about to go up on the auction block? Was she gambling on the chance that a local buyer might scoop her husband up, allowing them to remain together? Or was she simply so consumed by the emotions of giving birth that she couldn't get her head around the sheer impossibility of her husband's predicament—that he could either run today or be sold the day after tomorrow. He would almost certainly be gone either way.

"Where are you going?" Mary asked.

Robert made up a weak story about hiring himself out as a laborer the next day. With the Christmas holiday at hand, no farmers in the area would be doing any last-minute hiring. He walked out after telling that fib, but he came back into the cabin at the sound of his wife's tears. Mary saw that he remained as restless as ever.

> "Oh [Robert]! You're going to leave me! But wherever you go, remember me and the children."

He left again, this time for good. I find it impossible to imagine what might have been going on in his heart as he made his way through a driving rain storm, desperately trying to catch up with his sister and brothers before they departed Poplar Neck, where his parents had a one-room cabin.

Robert's love affair with Mary may have been ending that night, but another affair would move forward into freedom at the same time. After getting word that his sister Harriet was coming, Ben Ross set about bringing Jane Kane along on his run to freedom. He knew that it would be no easy feat for Jane to just up and walk away from property owned by a master as strict as Horatio Jones, so he set Jane up with a gender-bending disguise, arranging to have a new suit of men's clothes hidden somewhere in a garden on the Jones farm.

The morning of Christmas Eve, Jane sneaked down to the garden and donned that change of clothes. Almost immediately, the news that she was missing spread through the farm, but no one on the lookout for her that day caught on to the fact that the well-dressed young man who came strolling up from Buttons Creek and then walked right past the farm might be anything other than he appeared to be.

POSTSCRIPT
The End of the Affairs

Jane Kane and Ben Ross did find a measure of happily ever after in freedom, but it was short-lived. They were married in St. Catharine's, Ontario, where they took the adopted names of James and Catherine Stewart. They had a son, Elijah, and a daughter, Hester. Ben/James died young, however, in 1862 or 1863. Jane/Catherine would move to upstate New York, eventually, where she would remarry and have a third child before becoming a widow for a second time. In the census of 1870, she was described as a "servant."

The night their little Harriet was born was probably the last time Robert and Mary ever saw each other. A couple of historians have speculated that Mary and her children were the targets of a later Tubman rescue mission, but by that point Mary had been moved to another farm in another town. She had remarried by this point as well, and she was pregnant again.

I haven't come across any definitive account of what became of the infant Harriet, but I can say that Robert kept the promise he made to Mary on the night he left, that he would remember their children. After the end of the Civil War and the abolition of slavery, their boys John and Moses found themselves trapped in a complicated apprenticeship program that had been rejiggered by a white farmer back in Maryland to work pretty much like slavery did, only without the name.

Once he got wind of this, Robert (who took the name John Stewart in freedom) called on an old friend for help. That friend, John Bowley, liberated the boys from that farm and helped them make it up to Auburn, New York, where they were reunited with their father.

TESTIMONY
'Why Does the Slave Ever Love?'

Harriet Jacobs wrote one of the most dramatic slave narratives, *Incidents in the Life of a Slave Girl*. The book details her odyssey through a sexual harassment ordeal at the hands of a depraved, obsessive master and into an astonishing stretch of seven years spent hiding from him in a cramped attic while waiting for the chance to flee her native North Carolina. At one point in the book, she looks back with great sadness at the adolescent memory of the first genuine inkling of love she ever felt toward a young boy.

Why does the slave ever love? Why allow the tendrils of the heart to twine around objects which may at any moment be wrenched away by the hand of violence? When separations come by the hand of death, the pious soul can bow in resignation, and say, "Not my will, but thine be done, O Lord!" But when the ruthless hand of man strikes the blow, regardless of the misery he causes, it is hard to be submissive. I did not reason thus when I was a young girl. Youth will be youth. I loved and I indulged the hope that the dark clouds around me would turn out a bright lining. I forgot that in the land of my birth the shadows are too dense for light to penetrate.

Jacobs found her way to freedom eventually, and lived to the age of 83. The inscription on her headstone at Mount Auburn Cemetery in Cambridge, Massachusetts says, "Patient in tribulation, fervent in spirit serving the Lord."

CONNECTIONS

- I have split the famed Christmas Escape into three parts. The first part is in Chapter 5. The second part is this chapter. The third part is in Chapter 14.
- Long before he rescued Robert Ross's children after the Civil War, John Bowley had joined forces with Harriet Tubman to rescue his wife, Kessiah, and

their children from the auction block in Cambridge. That story is in Chapter 2.

TRAVEL RESOURCES

There is nothing in the way of gas or food along the route I have outlined between Stewart's Canal/Parsons Creek and the pull-off at the Little Blackwater River. There is only spectacular marshland scenery. Not to worry: Clean restrooms are available at the stops in each of the next two chapters.

Information about things to do and places to go in and around Dorchester County is available from **Dorchester County Tourism**.

- Dorchester Visitor Center, 2 Rose Hill Place, Cambridge, Maryland
- VisitDorchester.org; Facebook.com/DorchesterCounty; 410.228.1000

The **Harriet Tubman Underground Railroad Byway** runs through both Dorchester and Caroline counties in Maryland and then on into Delaware.

- Maryland: HarrietTubmanByway.org; Facebook.com/HarrietTubmanByway; 410.228.1000
- Delaware: TubmanBywayDelaware.org

8: The View North at the Harriet Tubman Underground Railroad Visitor Center

Dorchester County, Maryland

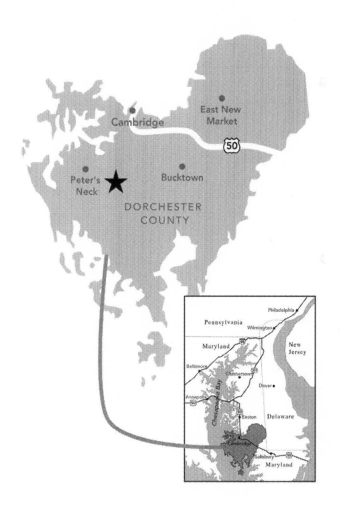

BIG PICTURE
Harriet Tubman's Posthumous Journey

Today, there is no serious question about Harriet Tubman's place in history. Her standing as an American hero of the first order is as secure as can be.

This wasn't always the case. When Tubman started out working along the Underground Railroad, she did so in complete anonymity, of course. But she gained a good measure of fame later in her own lifetime. A pair of biographies by her friend Sarah Bradford got the ball rolling. In her older years, at meetings of the women's suffrage movement, Tubman was treated as something akin to a rock star.

After her death in 1913 in her early 90s, Tubman slowly dropped back into obscurity. By the middle years of the 20th century, she was mainly in the public eye as a character in highly fictionalized books for children. Her journey back to prominence has come only in recent decades, along a road paved with the work of a few dedicated historians and supported by growing public interest in the history of both women and African Americans. (If I had to recommend just one of the newer Tubman biographies, it would be *Bound for the Promised Land* by Kate Clifford Larson.)

The exhibit materials in the first-rate facility that we are visiting in this chapter—it opened in the spring of 2017—were put together on the foundation of the work of these historians. While called a "Visitor Center," it feels more like a museum. Carrying the imprimatur of both the state of Maryland and the federal government, it represents another giant step in Tubman's posthumous journey back into the front ranks of American history.

STORY

The View North at the Harriet Tubman Underground Railroad Visitor Center

The architect Chris Elcock first visited the site of the Harriet Tubman Underground Railroad Visitor Center on Maryland's Eastern Shore in July of 2008, nearly a decade before the facility would open. He had come across the Chesapeake Bay Bridge from Baltimore that day in order to help decide whether his firm, GWWO Architects, would throw its hat in the ring as a candidate to design the facility being planned jointly by the National Park Service and the Maryland Department of Natural Resources.

Located just north of the Little Blackwater River along Route 335 (Golden Hill Road), the site covers 17 acres and sits smack dab in the middle of the landscape where the early part of Tubman's life unfolded. She spent most of those younger years living in either Peter's Neck, just to the northwest, or in Bucktown, just to the east.

The scene Elcock took in on that first visit amounted to a typical stretch of Eastern Shore countryside. Grasses swayed in the foreground. Off in the distance were stands of trees, glimpses of waterways, and swaths of corn and other farm crops. Eagles and osprey soared overhead. The place was thick with midsummer bugs. The only structure on the site then was an old farmhouse, and it was slated for demolition.

A woman standing near Elcock surveyed that scene and said in a tone of dismay, "There's nothing here."

Elcock had a different reaction. He felt like he was looking out over a landscape chock full of stories, drama, and meaning. In his mind's eye, he could see slaves on the run, making their way through those distant trees along the Underground Railroad. He could see others, too, the ones who decided to stay put, as they worked in nearby fields.

He tried to imagine the details of their lives, to place himself in their shoes and get a sense for what might have been in their hearts and heads. What fears, hopes, doubts, and misgivings did they harbor while trying to decide whether to stay at home or make a run for it?

"When she said that," Elcock said during a community presentation shortly before the facility opened, "it was all I could do to keep quiet." He is no longer feeling a need to stay silent. Not only did GWWO win the job, the firm put Elcock in charge of the 12-member team that designed the visitor center.

The first step in that design process involved drawing up an array of possible big-picture plans for the site. The winning concept had the title "The View North," because of the way it has visitors entering at the site's southern edge, then making their way into the exhibit area and following the story of the Underground Railroad along a cone-shaped route that opens up gradually as they move through the facility in a northward direction, toward freedom.

"If you really commit to the story you're telling, it ends up driving all of your decisions," Elcock said.

On first glance, the visitor center has a modest profile. Approaching it on Route 335, visitors see a run of four barn-like shapes built on a scale and in a style that fits in pretty well with the buildings on nearby farms. One of those shapes is dotted with rectangular windows arrayed in an intriguingly random pattern. Elcock explained how the light from those windows would be used to illuminate an exhibit area inside devoted to Tubman's spirituality.

The three large exhibit areas that make up the interior of the center were empty on the day I saw Elcock's presentation. They have since been filled in, of course, and they unfold just as he described, in a series of "stations." Visitors start out in relatively tight quarters on the south end of the space and then find more and more breathing room and natural light as they move northward and get deeper into the exhibits, which cover every period of Tubman's life.

The exhibits are quite well done, especially when driven by striking works of art, such as the larger-than-life wall painting of a young Harriet singing a farewell song to a friend as she gets ready to make her run for freedom. A three-dimensional piece showing Tubman reaching out a hand from the prow of a small boat to help slaves swimming for freedom is quite a showpiece as well.

Other touches are subtler. Along one corridor, overhead lights are set on the ceiling in a random pattern, so as to evoke the stars in the night sky that many slaves on the run used to find their way north.

Eventually, visitors need to turn around in the space and head back south to get back to the front door. The way Elcock sees it, this turn, too, echoes the stories of Tubman's life, given the way she decided to return south time and again in the face of great danger in order to help loved ones make their journey to freedom.

The center was designed to remain a work in progress for quite a few years after its opening. In time, an expansive "memorial garden" will grow in and take shape on the exterior grounds, looping around the northern end of the visitor center and changing with the passing seasons. I have heard that there are plans to commission and install a major piece of sculpture outside the center as well.

Elcock said he envisions another transformation, too, this one involving the zinc panels that cover much of the exterior of the exhibit buildings. "Zinc will dull over time," he explained. "It will take on something that is like a healing patina. What we hope, of course, is that that's just what happens over time to attitudes in this country about slavery and race."

The architects on Elcock's team spent countless hours engrossed in all of the various books that have been written about Tubman and the Underground Railroad. That experience, he said, left them all in awe of the woman whose life the new center strives to honor.

"This is a short woman—she is five-foot-nothing, and she weighs a hundred-and-nothing," he said. "She has epilepsy—this is the story of a woman with a disability, too. And she is illiterate. And she is a slave. But she made a change in the world, didn't she?"

TRAVEL RESOURCES

The **Harriet Tubman Underground Railroad Visitor Center** is at 4068 Golden Hill Road, Church Creek, Maryland.

- nps.gov/hatu; 410.221.2290

Information about things to do and places to go in and around Dorchester County is available from **Dorchester County Tourism**.

- Dorchester Visitor Center, 2 Rose Hill Place, Cambridge, Maryland
- VisitDorchester.org; Facebook.com/DorchesterCounty; 410.228.1000

The **Harriet Tubman Underground Railroad Byway** runs through both Dorchester and Caroline counties in Maryland and then on into Delaware.

- Maryland: HarrietTubmanByway.org; Facebook.com/HarrietTubmanByway; 410.228.1000
- Delaware: TubmanBywayDelaware.org

9: 'THE LORD GIVETH, AND THE LORD TAKETH AWAY'

Dorchester County, Maryland

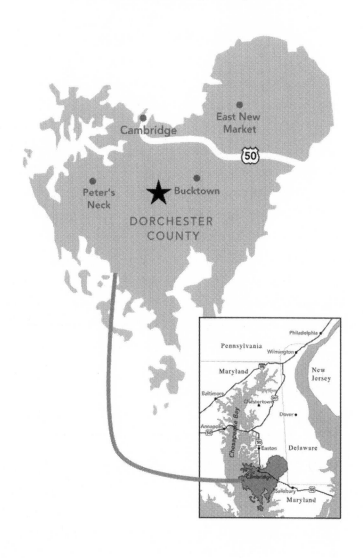

BIG PICTURE
'I Never Lost a Passenger'

I was the conductor of the Underground Railroad for eight years, and I can say what most conductors can't say; I never ran my train off the track, and I never lost a passenger.

Harriet Tubman was a celebrity and well into her 70s at the time she uttered this famous bit of braggadocio. She delivered the line in 1896, during a women's suffrage convention, and it must have brought down the house. And Lord knows, Tubman had earned every last bit of the applause she received that day.

But I can't help but wonder: Did the image of her sister Rachel come to her mind while she was basking in that applause? Did she maybe have a flashback to a snowy night spent alone in the woods, frozen and heartbroken and trying to come to grips with the fact that Rachel would never rejoin the family in freedom?

STORY
'The Lord Giveth, and the Lord Taketh Away'

We don't know the location of the patch of woods where Harriet Tubman endured the worst heartbreak of her time on the Underground Railroad, so we will have to make due with something nearby. We are in luck there: The entrance to Wildlife Drive at Blackwater National

Wildlife Refuge is a couple of miles down Key Wallace Drive from our last stop at the Harriet Tubman Underground Railroad Visitor Center.

Take your time entering Wildlife Drive and soak in the view of the Little Blackwater River. Stay to your left at the first opportunity and then turn into the parking area for a short, easy walking loop called the Marsh Edge Trail.

This little pocket of woods stands between the two places Harriet Tubman knew best in her younger years. Peter's Neck lies to the northwest. She was born there as Araminta Ross, and she returned there during her adolescence. The village of Bucktown, where she spent the years in between, is over to the east.

This was the landscape where young Araminta, or "Minty," endured the pain of her family being torn apart. She lost three older sisters, all sold away to slave traders from the Deep South. Two of those sisters were young mothers, and the sales separated them from their children.

Minty eventually took the name Harriet Tubman, of course. As a conductor on the Underground Railroad, she rescued about 70 people over the course of 13 trips back into slave territory. Some were strangers. Some were acquaintances. Some were family.

Everyone who knew Tubman well understood that this last group was the raison d'être of her work. By the time of her last mission in 1860, she had made a lot of progress in bringing her family out of bondage. All four of her brothers were free. She had saved her parents in the nick of time, just before her father's likely arrest for his work as an Underground Railroad station master. Her niece, Kessiah, was living in Canada now, too. (As the daughter of one of her lost sisters, Kessiah ranked as something of an honorary sibling.)

A few nieces, nephews, and other close relatives remained in bondage, but there was just one last sibling, Rachel. This younger sister became something of a holy grail for Harriet over the years. The letters and journals of Underground Railroad compatriots such as Thomas Garrett and William Still are dotted with mentions of how Harriet was working on this, that, or another plan for rescuing her sister.

On one earlier occasion, Tubman had come tantalizingly close to success. She had returned to Dorchester County and gotten a message to her sister through the Underground Railroad grapevine that it was time to run. But Rachel refused to go. Her children had been hired out to work on another farm, and there was no way to retrieve them in time. She wasn't going to leave those kids behind.

This complication was probably more than a coincidence. Rachel was still owned by the Brodess family, and that family had by this point seen five of the Ross siblings run away. Rachel must have been regarded as a high flight risk. The decision to keep her apart from her children was likely a strategic one, aimed at discouraging her from running.

By 1860, the Eastern Shore was more dangerous than ever for conductors like Tubman. A rash of slave escapes in the mid-1850s had sparked a furious reaction from slave owners, who demanded that sheriffs and prosecutors crack down on anyone helping the runaways. Those owners had also begun keeping a closer watch over their "property," and paying more attention the comings and goings of strangers on area roads and rivers.

It was around this time that Thomas Garrett started expressing uncharacteristic concerns about Tubman's safety.

> There is now much more risk on the road ... than has been for several months past, as we find that poor, worthless wretches are constantly on the look out on two roads that [Harriet] cannot well avoid, especially with carriage, yet, as it is Harriet, who seems to have had a special angel to guard her on her journey of mercy, I have hope.

The trip Tubman took back to the Eastern Shore that December would be her 13th and final mission. The sequence of events and some details about what happened on this trip south remain a little unclear, but this much is for sure: Upon arriving in Dorchester County, Harriet learned that her sister Rachel had died—she was only about 35 years old. There is nothing definitive that I have seen about what sort of illness or incident ended her life.

Even now, in the midst of her shock and grief, Tubman managed somehow to pull herself together. It seems likely that she at least looked into the possibility of rescuing Rachel's children, Ben and Angerine, but the logistics proved impossible.

In later years, a bit of oral history among Tubman's friends and family surfaced claiming that Harriet had to leave Rachel's children behind "for want of $30." Presumably, this is a reference to the funds she needed to pay a bribe or hire a wagon or meet some other necessity.

In Sarah Bradford's biography of Tubman, there is an especially harrowing anecdote that Harriet herself places during her "last journey." The timing remains a bit unclear in the larger and somewhat jumbled context of the book, but if it did indeed occur during this 1860 trip, then it must have happened after she received the news about Rachel.

Harriet is alone in a stand of woods like the one here at the Marsh Edge Trail, and she is awaiting the arrival of an unnamed party of fugitives. It's possible, but far from certain, that this group was supposed to include Ben and Angerine. In any case, the fugitives fail to show.

The weather takes a dreadful turn, the wind whipping things up into a driving snowstorm. This forces Tubman to seek the only smidgen of shelter she can find, behind a tree trunk. There she sits the whole night through, alone and shivering and grieving the loss of her sister.

The next day is when Tubman pulled herself together. She received word along the grapevine that a couple named Stephen and Maria Ennals were ready to run with their three children. Their youngest was just three months old.

That grew into a party of seven when another man, known only as John, joined in the escape. From the get-go, things did not go well. That snowstorm of the night before had given way to freezing rain. Eventually, Harriet came up to a house that had long served as an Underground Railroad station and gave a coded knock at the door.

A white man appeared at the window and told Tubman that the black man she had expected to find there had been "obliged to leave" over suspicions that he was helping runaway slaves.

Day was breaking. Nearby roads were being watched. The white man at the window might well report her visit to the authorities. Two of the Ennals children were being drugged so that they would remain quiet. Without that station master, Tubman's party was in a dreadful bind.

People like me who write about Tubman's life often end up going over the top and making her seem like some sort of superwoman, always able to reach down inside and come up with one clever trick or another to save the day.

This time, Tubman had nothing up her sleeve. She decided to retreat, finding her way to a nearby stretch of marsh that had a little patch of high land. She told her frozen, hungry, and exhausted party to wade through the water and climb up onto that island. There, they would be able keep out of sight in the "tall and rank" grasses.

Even here, however, Tubman sensed danger in the extreme. She decided that she couldn't risk going back out on her own in search of much-needed food and supplies. That left only one option: Prayer.

> Her faith never wavered, her silent prayer still ascended, and she confidently expected help from some quarter or other.

Those words are from Bradford's biography again. Bradford goes on in that book to tell how the group spent that whole long day laying in the grass and waiting for an answer to Harriet's prayers. Then, shortly after dusk, the answer came in the form of a white man who appeared along a path on the mainland.

Tubman had no idea who this man was, but she could see that he was dressed like a Quaker. At first, she thought he was just mumbling to himself, but then she was able to catch a couple of words and, eventually, make out the message that he was repeating over and over.

> My wagon stands in the barn-yard of the farm across the way; the horse is in the stable; the harness hangs on a nail.

When night fell, Tubman waded back through the water and climbed onto the mainland. The wagon she found on that man's farm had been fitted out generously with food and supplies. She and her six runaways were soon riding through the darkness to another station that Harriet knew in another town. This station would turn out to be still intact.

In later years, Tubman would say that she never figured out who that man with the wagon was or how he came to know that she and her runaways were hiding on that island. Here is Bradford again:

> But these sudden deliverances never seemed to strike her as at all strange or mysterious; her prayer was the prayer of faith, and she *expected* an answer.

Somewhere along the way on this final trip, Tubman picked up an extra runaway. By Christmas, a friend of Tubman's in Auburn, NY, was reporting in a letter to her daughter that she had been congratulating Harriet for the "seven newly arrived slaves" but also extending "our sympathies" over the heartbreaking news about Rachel.

TESTIMONY
Frederick Douglass on Harriet Tubman

Modern-day book readers know what to expect to see on the back cover of a book. That is the place where authors tend to put laudatory quotes from other writers and famous friends, in hopes of selling a few more copies.

This same sort of thing was going on in the 1800s, but in a different fashion. Back then, letters of recommendation from VIP types were reprinted inside the book in order to assure readers that the author and her subject matter were worthy of their attention.

When Sarah Bradford was getting ready to publish the first of her Tubman biographies, she or someone else involved in the project asked Frederick Douglass if he would provide a letter attesting to the character of Harriet Tubman. The letter that Douglass soon sent along is, for my money, the greatest letter of reference in the history of the world.

Dear Harriet:

I am glad to know that the story of your eventful life has been written by a kind lady, and that the same is soon to be published. You ask for what you do not need when you call upon me for a word of commendation. I need such words from you far more than you can need them from me, especially where your superior labors and devotion to the cause of the lately enslaved of our land are known as I know them.

The difference between us is very marked. Most that I have done and suffered in the service of our cause has been in public, and I have received much encouragement at every step of the way.

You, on the other hand, have labored in a private way. I have wrought in the day—you in the night. I have had the applause of the crowd and the satisfaction that comes of being approved by the multitude, while the most that you have done has been witnessed by a few trembling, scarred, and foot-sore bondmen and women, whom you have led out of the house of bondage, and whose heartfelt, "God bless you," has been your only reward.

The midnight sky and the silent stars have been the witnesses of your devotion to freedom and of your heroism. Excepting John Brown—of sacred memory—I know of no one who has willingly encountered more perils and hardships to serve our enslaved people than you have.

Much that you have done would seem improbable to those who do not know you as I know you. It is to me a great pleasure and a great privilege to bear testimony for your character and your works, and to say to those to whom you may come, that I regard you in every way truthful and trustworthy.

Your friend,

Frederick Douglass

CONNECTIONS

- The full story of the earlier mission when Rachel Ross refused to run away with Tubman because she wouldn't leave her children behind is in Chapter 32.
- The story of how Tubman rescued her three brothers in the Christmas Escape of 1854 is told in three parts: Chapter 5, Chapter 7, and Chapter 14.
- The story of how Harriet helped her parents to flee from Poplar Neck in the nick of time is in Chapter 15.
- The story of Tubman's role in the escape that Kessiah Bowley made straight from a slave auction block is in Chapter 2.

TRAVEL RESOURCES

Blackwater National Wildlife Refuge has a visitor center at 2145 Key Wallace Drive in Cambridge, Maryland. There, you will find restroom facilities, nature exhibits, and a gift shop.
- FriendsofBlackwater.org; 410.228.2677

Information about things to do and places to go in and around Dorchester County is available from **Dorchester County Tourism**.
- Dorchester Visitor Center, 2 Rose Hill Place, Cambridge, Maryland

- VisitDorchester.org;
  Facebook.com/DorchesterCounty; 410.228.1000

The **Harriet Tubman Underground Railroad Byway** runs through both Dorchester and Caroline counties in Maryland and then on into Delaware.

- Maryland: HarrietTubmanByway.org;
  Facebook.com/HarrietTubmanByway;
  410.228.1000
- Delaware: TubmanBywayDelaware.org

10: Young Harriet Goes Down to the Crossroads

Bucktown, Maryland

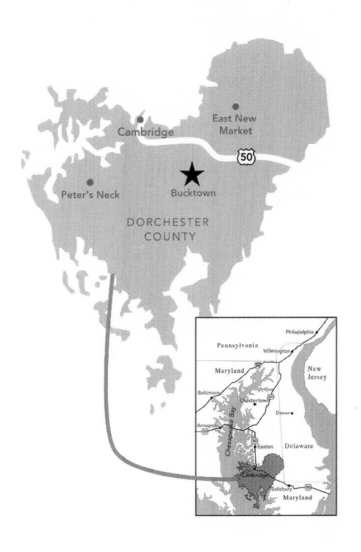

BIG PICTURE
God Works in Mysterious Ways

The old truism in this headline will likely end up first and foremost in your mind on a visit to the little Bucktown Village Store, which stands at the isolated crossroads of Greenbriar, Bucktown, and Bestpitch Ferry roads in the heart of Dorchester County, Maryland.

Do you know the legend about the old-time bluesman Robert Johnson? He is the one who supposedly went down to a "Cross Road" and sold his soul to the devil in exchange for the ability to play the guitar like no one else. Sometimes I think of this crossroads in Bucktown as the other side of that coin. This is where Harriet Tubman found her God, and they would develop quite a relationship over time. Here is the famous Underground Railroad station master Thomas Garrett on that topic:

> I never met with any person, of any color, who had more confidence in the voice of God, as spoken direct to her soul. [Harriet] has frequently told me that she talked with God, and he talked with her, every day of her life.

Faith is a topic of paramount importance in the story of Harriet Tubman. Hers was a religion of the up-close-and-visceral variety, full of intense visions and strange voices and sudden losses of consciousness. Asked later in life why she made this or that or another fortuitous decision while leading her charges to freedom, Tubman would invariably respond that it was God telling her what to do, every step of the way.

The story of what happened to young Harriet at the Bucktown store raises some questions that are, in the end, unanswerable. Were the visions Harriet saw and the voices she heeded really gifts from God? Or were they instead the result of an illness brought on by the brain injury she suffered at these crossroads? Or were they, perhaps, a bit of both?

STORY
Young Harriet Goes Down to the Crossroads

The Bucktown Village Store isn't much to look at, really. It's small and squat, with plain weatherboard siding and a basic wood-shingled roof. Nor is there all that much to do in the general vicinity, outside of wandering some backroads and taking in the scenery.

But this place is quite special when it comes to Underground Railroad wanderings. Most buildings that survive today from back in Tubman's time are glittery affairs—mansions, courthouses, and churches. This store is different: It's a tangible remnant of the day-to-day routine of people in the days of slavery. It's a place where the squeaking of the floorboards can feel like an echo from the past. It's a place where you can really feel like you're walking in Tubman's footsteps.

There was definitely a store at this crossroads in the 1830s, and that store was definitely the site of a key event in Tubman's life. Experts tend to date the walls of this particular building to a smidge or two later, while leaving a little wiggle room for uncertainty. One decent bet is that an earlier, 1830s store stood exactly on the foundation of this current building, which means that, yes, those footsteps you sense are the real deal.

Tubman's name at birth was Araminta Ross. "Minty" was still a baby when her owner, Edward Brodess, turned 21 years old and assumed legal ownership of his human property. He promptly had Harriet's mother pack up her children and move from the cabin in Peter's Neck, where Minty had been born, to Bucktown, a distance of about 10 miles.

Minty's father, Ben Ross, had to stay behind with his owner, Anthony Thompson. (The family had been able to live together for a number of years before that because Thompson served as the legal guardian of the Brodess slaves while Edward was a minor.)

This miserable stretch of separation for the Rosses got worse shortly after the move to Bucktown, when Brodess sold off one of Minty's sisters, Mariah Ritty. No one would ever see her again.

As a young child, Minty landed in situations that can be hard for our modern-world minds to grasp. For instance, she insisted later in life that she was serving long days as the sole caretaker for younger siblings by the age of *five*.

It was late nights for my mother's git home, an' when [one of the babies would] get [to] worryin' I'd cut a fat chunk [of] pork an' toast it on de coals an' put it in his mouf. One night he went to sleep wid that hangin', an' when my mother came home she thought I'd done kill him.

Minty started getting hired out to neighboring farms and households before she turned 10. She was perhaps 11 or 12 on the day in the early 1830s when she and a fellow slave ventured out to the Bucktown store to pick up some supplies.

There, young Minty landed in the middle of quite a ruckus. A slave had run off his post on a nearby farm. An overseer was in hot pursuit and caught up with him at the store. That overseer asked Minty and several others for help in tying the young man down. Minty refused—as far as we know, this was the first public act of defiance against slavery by the girl who would grow up to become Harriet Tubman.

The young man managed to wriggle free and make a run for the door of the store. The overseer picked up a two-pound metal weight and threw it at the fleeing man. He missed his target. The weight struck Minty square in the head.

Minty was assigned in those days to the dirty job of breaking flax in the field. She hadn't combed her hair in forever. It stood out "like a bushel basket," and her embarrassment about that is why she covered her head with a shawl before going into the Bucktown store that day.

I expect that thar hair saved my life.

The weight crashed through her skull, driving pieces of the shawl deep into her head. By all accounts, she very nearly died. She was mostly worthless as a laborer for a period of recovery that stretched into years. Brodess tried to sell Minty during this period, but no one wanted to buy such a small and sickly girl.

Minty was never the same after that injury. She would gain the full measure of her physical strength back eventually, but her mind was changed forever. She developed a weird sleeping sickness, nodding off at unpredictable times into a hazy state of semi-consciousness. Friends and acquaintances throughout her long life would marvel over the way Tubman could nod off in mid-conversation, then snap out of it a few minutes later and finish off a thought or a sentence as if no time at all had passed.

Here is how Tubman's first biographer, Sarah Bradford, describes those episodes:

[W]hen these turns of somnolency come upon Harriet, she imagines that her "spirit" leaves her body, and visits other scenes and places, not only in this world, but in the world of spirits. And her ideas of these scenes show, to say the least of it, a vividness of imagination seldom equaled in the soarings of the most cultivated minds.

In addition to vivid dreams and strange visions, she started to hear strange voices as well in the wake of the Bucktown store incident. Over time, those visions and voices stopped feeling strange to Tubman and started to feel more like something that amounted to God's direct presence in her heart and head. On the Underground Railroad, she often followed paths laid out in accord with those visions and voices.

Tubman biographer Kate Larson did a neat bit of detective work on this seemingly strange turn of events. It turns out that these symptoms—the dreams, the voices, the sleeping sickness—all point to a medical condition called temporal lobe epilepsy (TLE), which can be caused by the kind of trauma to the head that Tubman suffered.

But that diagnosis still leaves unanswered in my mind some of the deeper questions raised by the workings of faith in Tubman's life. For Harriet, those voices and visions were manifestations of a faith that delivered the goods. When she asked God to give her a little extra strength or wisdom or trickery or good luck or financial assistance, well, she usually got it.

So whether or not the experts are right to give her a retrospective diagnosis of TLE, that doesn't change the way a visit to this crossroads in Bucktown will leave you thinking about the old truism: God works in mysterious ways.

TESTIMONY
'De Lord Is Nebber Mistaken'

On one of her later missions, Harriet Tubman set out to rescue her parents from their cabin on Poplar Neck, which is up in Caroline County, Maryland. She took on that mission after feeling one of those strange presentiments that she regarded as gifts from God. In this case, it was a nagging feeling that her parents, Ben and Rit Ross, might be in trouble.

As always, however, there were mundane affairs of the world to tend to while getting about God's work— money, for instance. Here is how Tubman's biographer, Sarah Bradford, describes the way she went about her fundraising on this particular campaign.

When ... she received an intimation in some mysterious or supernatural way that the old people were in trouble and needed her, she asked the Lord where she should go for the money to enable her to go for them.

She was in some way, as she supposed, directed to the office of a certain gentleman, a friend of the slaves, in New York. When she left the house of the friends with whom she was staying, she said: "I'm gwine to Mr. ———'s office, an' I ain't gwine to lebe dere, an' I ain't gwine to eat or drink, till I get money enough to take me down after de ole people."

She went into this gentleman's office.

"How do you do, Harriet? What do you want?" was the first greeting.

"I want some money, sir."

"You do! How much do you want?"

"I want twenty dollars, sir!"

"Twenty dollars! Who told you to come here for twenty dollars!"

"De Lord tole me, sir."

"He did? Well I guess the Lord's mistaken this time."

"No, sir; de Lord is nebber mistaken! Anyhow I'm gwine to sit here till I get it."

So she sat down and went to sleep. All the morning, and all the afternoon, she sat there still; sometimes sleeping, sometimes rousing up, often finding the office full of gentlemen; sometimes finding herself alone. Many fugitives were passing through New York at this time, and those who came in supposed her to be one of them, tired out, and resting.

Sometimes she would be roused up with the words: "Come, Harriet! You had better go; there's no money for you here."

"No, sir; I'm not gwine to stir from here till I git my twenty dollars!"

She does not know all that happened, for deep sleep fell upon her; probably one of the turns of somnolency to which she has always been subject; but without doubt her story was whispered from one to another, and as her name and exploits were well known to many persons, the sympathies of some of those visitors to the office were aroused; at all events she came to full consciousness, at last, to find herself the happy possessor of sixty dollars, the contribution of these strangers.

She went on her way rejoicing to bring her old parents from the land of bondage.

CONNECTIONS

- The story of Harriet Tubman's birth in Peter's Neck and early childhood in Bucktown is in Chapter 4.
- The story of Tubman's physical recovery from the injuries she suffered at the Bucktown store is in Chapter 6.
- The story of how Tubman came back to rescue her parents when her father was about to be arrested is in Chapter 15.

TRAVEL RESOURCES

The **Bucktown Village Store** is owned by The Bucktown Foundation, a tiny nonprofit led by Jay and Susan Meredith, a local couple who have worked tirelessly to preserve the building. You can always stop by and check out the exterior, but if you want to go inside it's best to call in advance.

- 4303 Bucktown Road, Cambridge, Maryland
- BlackwaterPaddleandPedal.com; 410.901.9255

- The web address above is for another business the Merediths run, and it means that they can also help with your bicycle or kayak needs.

Information about things to do and places to go in and around Dorchester County is available from **Dorchester County Tourism**.

- Dorchester Visitor Center, 2 Rose Hill Place, Cambridge, Maryland
- VisitDorchester.org; Facebook.com/DorchesterCounty; 410.228.1000

The **Harriet Tubman Underground Railroad Byway** runs through both Dorchester and Caroline counties in Maryland and then on into Delaware.

- Maryland: HarrietTubmanByway.org; Facebook.com/HarrietTubmanByway; 410.228.1000
- Delaware: TubmanBywayDelaware.org

11: The Price of Freedom

East New Market, Maryland

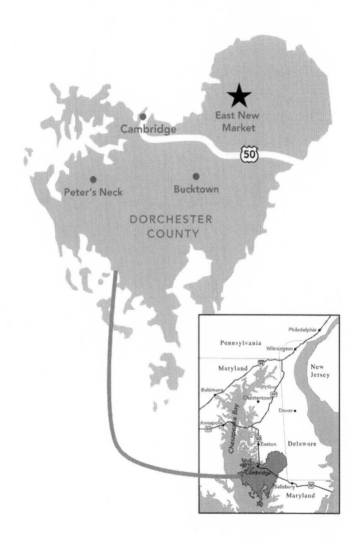

BIG PICTURE
Another Way Out of Bondage

Samuel Green was born a slave in 1802, most likely in the area of Indian Creek, a crescent-shaped swath of water located off of the Choptank River near the town of East New Market, Maryland. The name of that creek is no accident; neither is the name of nearby Indian Grant Road. This territory once belonged to the Nanticoke Indians, and there are threads in the historical record hinting that Green many have had a mixed-race ancestry that included Indian blood.

The Indian Creek area was also the childhood stomping grounds of a future Maryland governor, Thomas Holliday Hicks. He was born a few years before Green, but it's quite possible that their paths crossed in childhood. Their paths would cross again—quite famously—in the 1850s, after Green had landed in prison and his case had become something of a cause célèbre among abolitionists all around the country.

The route Samuel Green took to freedom did not involve the Underground Railroad. Not much is known about Green's younger years. The guesswork among historians is that he was a farmworker of some sort. By the time he reached his late 20s he was the property of a landowner named Henry Nichols.

By then, Green had married an enslaved woman named Catherine. Everyone called her "Kitty." They had two children, Sam Jr. and Sarah.

Kitty and the children belonged to a different owner, Ezekiel Richardson, but it seems that the Greens managed to work things out between the two owners so that all four of them lived in the same household around East New Market for most, if not all, of the children's younger years.

When Nichols died in 1832, his will stipulated that Samuel Green would need to put in five more years working as a slave, but he would become a free man after that. Such "manumissions" were not rare—quite a few blacks on the Eastern Shore found their way to freedom in the manner of Samuel Green, rather than along the Underground Railroad.

- In 1800, there were 105,000 slaves in Maryland, compared with 20,000 free blacks.
- In 1860, there were 87,000 slaves in Maryland, compared with 84,000 free blacks.

Not all of that jump in the number of free blacks was due to manumission. There were other factors at work, including a surge in self-liberation by blacks who cobbled together enough money to buy freedom for themselves and/or their loved ones. Nonetheless, here is one bit of big-picture perspective on those population numbers:

- The number of slaves who escaped along the Underground Railroad all over the country between 1800 and 1865 is estimated at about 100,000, on the high end.

- In roughly that same window, the state of Maryland alone saw an increase in its number of free blacks of 64,000.

There is an important caveat to this, however: "Free" blacks back then weren't really free, in the modern-day sense. They couldn't vote. They weren't allowed to press criminal charges or testify in court against white people. They had to carry identification papers and be ready to prove themselves at every turn to authorities and bounty hunters. Such a list of the indignities and injustices suffered by these "free" blacks could go on and on.

There are no surviving hints in the record as to why Nichols decided to free Samuel Green. He may have been motivated by religious conviction. Several Methodist ministers on the Eastern Shore were preaching in those years about manumission in the context of Christian charity and God's will. But religion wasn't the only motive involved. Some owners freed slaves for personal reasons—as a reward for loyal service, for example. Others did so for pragmatic reasons related to the various legal and accounting advice they got while managing the affairs of their businesses and estates. Still others did so selfishly, so they wouldn't have to provide housing and care for older slaves who were no longer productive workers.

Within a year or so of Nichols's death, Green had saved up enough money to buy off the last few years of his bondage. He was still a young man, about 30 years of age, when he became free. A couple of years later, he engaged in a little self-liberation and bought Kitty's freedom, too. When it comes to Sam Jr. and Sarah, however, that's another story.

STORY
The Price of Freedom

The most popular route from Dorchester County into Delaware along the Underground Railroad ran through Samuel Green's old stomping grounds. Just below East New Market today, there is a route-number switcheroo to look out for. Route 16 veers off to the north, into the historic downtown area and then up toward Preston. The road that stays straight becomes Route 392 and reaches an intersection with Railroad Avenue as it runs through town.

Faith Community United Methodist Church is tucked off to the east there, behind the tracks that give that road its name. The church dates its history to 1844, when it was known as Colored People's United Methodist. As an adult, Samuel Green served as a minister here. He also operated a station along the Underground Railroad, presumably out of the cabin nearby where he and Kitty lived.

By all indications, Green was a decent, well-liked man. By the 1840s he seems to have developed a good reputation in the community among blacks and whites alike. It's not clear how he came to learn to read and write, but somewhere along the line he did, a rarity for blacks of his day.

Slavery was a matrilineal affair, with ownership of children passing through the mother at birth. That's how Ezekiel Richardson came to own Sam Jr. and Sarah even after Samuel and Kitty Green became free. Richardson eventually sold the Green children to a man named Dr. James Muse, who moved them out of their parents' home and into his house on prestigious High Street in Cambridge, Maryland, about 10 miles away. That house, now known as the 1849 Muse-Goldsborough House, is still standing today at 111 High Street.

Interestingly, Samuel and Kitty did not have an empty household for long during this period. By the time of the 1850 census, they had taken in a couple of strays—their household is listed with two children who were not their own, one a mulatto and the other black.

Down in Cambridge, Sam Jr. found himself in a bad situation. Years later, he would talk about having seen "whipping and all manner of cruelty inflicted [by Muse] upon his servants." In the late summer of 1854, Sam Jr. decided that he had had enough. He got word up to East New Market:

Father, I must fly for freedom!

The elder Samuel would eventually come up with a beautiful turn of phrase to describe what Sam Jr. was up to in the act of escaping to the North:

He prayed with his legs.

Young Sam Jr. made it to Canada in reasonably short order. Here is the text of a letter he wrote to his parents in September 1854:

I take this opportunity to Rite you a few lines to let you know how I am. I am well at present. I hope you and mother and all the famlay are the same. I arived to Canaday on 5 of Sep and I Got into Work as soon as I gat thar in a Saw Mill. ... I had it very plesent all of my travel plenty of friends plenty to eat and drink. ... I have got a grat dele to say but hav not time now give my love to all the friends and the woman, tell P. Jackson to come on Joseph Baily com on, Kom more. I remain yours til dath Samuel Green.

What happened next back home in Maryland must have torn Sam Jr. apart. His sister Sarah was a married woman by this point, with two young children. Shortly after Sam Jr.'s escape, her owner, James Muse, ripped that young family apart, selling Sarah—and only Sarah—to an owner in Missouri. No one knows what became of her after that.

Meanwhile, Samuel Sr. was becoming an ever more prominent member of the Dorchester County community. In 1852, he was selected as a representative to a statewide "Convention of the Free Colored People of Maryland." In 1855, he attended the

National Convention of the Colored People of the United States in Philadelphia. Many prominent black abolitionists were there, including Frederick Douglass.

Somewhere around this time, Green made a trip to Canada and visited with Sam Jr. While there, he decided that he and Kitty would move to Canada someday soon and join their son.

Green was probably running an Underground Railroad station through this whole period. Harriet Tubman seemed to know about Green, and to trust him. A couple of historians have speculated that Sam Jr. made his run to Canada bearing instructions from Tubman herself.

The elder Green almost certainly provided a safe haven in March 1857 to a group of Dorchester County runaways who would come to be known as the Dover Eight, after a miraculous moonlight escape out of the jailhouse in the capital city of Delaware. Their flight, and the publicity it engendered, set off a frenzy among slave owners in Dorchester County. They demanded something, anything, be done to stem the flow of runaways and protect their property rights.

That's why Dorchester County Sheriff Robert Bell came knocking at Samuel Green's door with a warrant on April 4.

"Come in, sir," Green told him. "It is a small cottage. You can soon search it through, but you will find nothing, for there is nothing to find."

Bell did find a few things, though the items sound rather innocuous to our modern ears. There was that letter from Green's son, a runaway, along with maps and train schedules showing the way to Canada. In addition, Bell found a copy of the novel *Uncle Tom's Cabin*, which had been causing quite a stir since its publication in 1852.

To be honest, I have always been a little confused by what happened next. In much of my reading about slavery times, the legal system in pro-slavery places like Dorchester County is portrayed as a kangaroo-style affair through and through, with slaves always found guilty no matter how innocent they were and slave owners always found innocent no matter how guilty they were. There must be a good amount of truth in those portrayals of a rigged system: A mountain of reliable testimony by former slaves describes incidents where owners and overseers got away, quite literally, with murder.

But those portrayals also must be a bit of an oversimplification, given what happened in the first trial of Samuel Green. It was a hard-fought affair, centered on those maps and train schedules for travel to Canada, but he was acquitted. (This verdict came even in a case where the court had appointed a defense attorney with a public record of expressing pro-slavery sympathies.)

In a second trial, this one focused on *Uncle Tom's Cabin*, Green did not fare as well. Found guilty under a law that made it illegal to possess material of an "inflammatory character" that might sow discontent or cause unrest among slaves, he was sentenced to 10 years in jail, the minimum allowed under the law. Green started serving his term at a prison in Baltimore City on May 18, 1857.

No one seems to know what became of Kitty during this period. Some historians have speculated that she might have been forced to sell the family belongings in order to pay for legal and living expenses. Others have wondered if she moved to Baltimore to be closer to her husband, or to Canada and the home of Sam Jr.

In short order, the story of Samuel Green's imprisonment became the talk of the nation. Newspaper reporters from near and far weighed in on the case of a supposedly free man imprisoned for having a copy of a best-selling book. Petition drives were taken up on Green's behalf—and not just by among the abolitionists of the North. Green had many supporters in Maryland who spoke up as well.

Maryland's governor at the time was Thomas Holliday Hicks, that fellow native of the Indian Creek area where Green had been born. A member of the colorfully named Know Nothing Party, Hicks was the sort of politician who toed a delicate line on the key issues of his day—he opposed secession and would later back Abraham Lincoln, but he also supported slavery and backed strong measures to protect the property rights of slave owners.

Hicks refused to pardon Green, or even to reduce his sentence. Green wouldn't catch a break until 1862, when Augustus Bradford took over as governor and commuted Green's sentence on condition that he leave the state within 60 days. On his way north, Green visited with William Still in Philadelphia. He also made an appearance at Shiloh Church in New York City, which was run by another famous Eastern Shore-born preacher, the former slave Henry Highland Garnet.

While in New York, Green paid a call on Harriet Beecher Stowe, the celebrated author of *Uncle Tom's Cabin*. All we know about that meeting comes from a short mention she gave it in a much longer newspaper article devoted mainly to other topics.

> There came a black man to our house a few days ago, who had spent five years at hard labor in a Maryland penitentiary for the crime of having a copy of *Uncle Tom's Cabin* in his house. He had been sentenced for ten years, but on his promise to leave the state and go to Canada, was magnanimously pardoned out ... and so he left Maryland without any acquisition except an infirmity of the limbs which he had caught from prison labor.
>
> All this was his portion of the cross; and he took it meekly, without comment, only asking that as they did not allow him to finish reading the book, would we give him a copy of *Uncle Tom's Cabin*, which we did.

Green lived out the rest of his days in relative obscurity. The 1870 census shows him back in the farm country of north Dorchester County, living in the vicinity of the intersection of Hicksburg Road and Route 16. By the time of his death in February 1877, he had been living in Baltimore City for a few years.

Kitty outlived her husband—she was still appearing in the community directories of Baltimore City as late as 1886. Sam Jr. seems to have remained in Canada for the rest of his days. Census records up there show him as a married father of two in the 1870s. He was working as a barber.

Most historians looking back at these events focus understandably on the elder Samuel Green and the injustice he suffered for owning a popular book. But my thoughts tend to stray toward his son, Sam Jr. Here is a young man who made a successful dash to freedom, something we tend to look back on now as a cause for celebration.

And yet, even in freedom, Sam Jr. found himself enduring heartbreaks rooted in the injustices of slavery. His sister was sold off and separated from her husband and children. His father was arrested, in part because of a letter Sam Jr. had sent simply to let his parents know that he was safe. It was with Sam Jr. in mind that I gave this story the title, "The Price of Freedom."

POSTSCRIPT
The Manumission that Wasn't

A man named Atthow Pattison looms large in the story of Harriet Tubman's roots on the Eastern Shore of Maryland. He purchased the Ashanti woman who came from West Africa aboard a slave ship and eventually took the name Modesty Green. Modesty gave birth to Harriet "Rit" Green, who would give birth in time to Araminta Ross, who the world would come to know as Harriet Tubman.

When Pattison died in 1797, this is what his will said:

I give and bequeath unto my Grand daughter, Mary Pattison, one negro girl called Rittia and her increase until she and they arrive to 45 years of age.

The implication is quite clear. Harriet Tubman's mother (and all of her children after her) were supposed to become free at the age of 45. The Pattison family seems to have simply gone about their affairs pretending that this provision in the will did not exist. They never got caught.

The family's slaves heard rumors about what was really in the will. While still a slave, Harriet Tubman managed to cobble together $5 and hire a lawyer to review the document.

Presumably, she learned that the rumors were true, but she didn't take any further legal action. Perhaps that decision was a simple matter of not having more funds to pay a lawyer to pursue the matter. Perhaps it was a case of not having any faith in the justice system of slavery times. Either way, the story of Atthow Pattison's will goes to show that manumissions didn't always unfold the way they were supposed to.

CONNECTIONS

- In the letter Sam Green Jr. sent to his father, he mentions "Joseph" Bailey and asks his father to tell him to "come on, kom more" to freedom. That is most likely a reference to Josiah Bailey, whose story is in Chapter 32.
- Samuel Green Sr. wasn't the only conductor on the Underground Railroad who became a target after slave owners began demanding local law enforcement officials clamp down on runaways and their helpers. Harriet Tubman's father, Ben Ross, also ended up in those crosshairs. That story is in Chapter 15.
- The Muse-Goldsborough House that Sam Jr. escaped from on High Street is quite close to the Cambridge sites associated with the stories in Chapter 1 and Chapter 2.

TRAVEL RESOURCES

Pretty downtown **East New Market** is mostly a residential affair, though there is a restaurant and a little shop or two located there. Similar small smatterings of amenities can be found in the nearby towns of **Hurlock** and **Secretary**.

Information about things to do and places to go in the area is available from **Dorchester County Tourism**.

- Dorchester Visitor Center, 2 Rose Hill Place, Cambridge, Maryland
- VisitDorchester.org; Facebook.com/DorchesterCounty; 410.228.1000

The **Harriet Tubman Underground Railroad Byway** runs through both Dorchester and Caroline counties in Maryland and then on into Delaware.

- Maryland: HarrietTubmanByway.org; Facebook.com/HarrietTubmanByway; 410.228.1000
- Delaware: TubmanBywayDelaware.org

12: Sailing *South* to Freedom

Seaford, Delaware

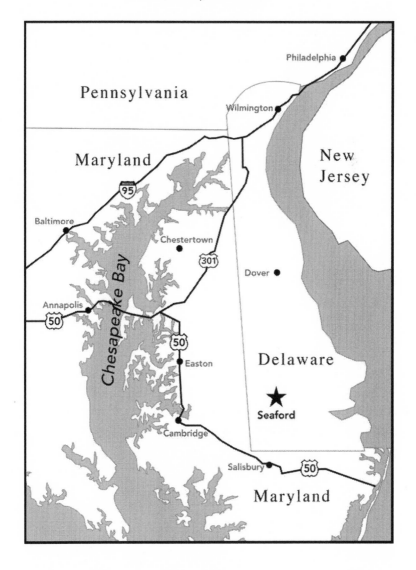

BIG PICTURE
Tricks of the Trade

Back during the Ottoman Empire, a German military commander named Helmuth von Moltke came up with a turn of phrase that has been a go-to aphorism in military circles for centuries now. It goes like this: "No battle plan survives contact with the enemy."

This bit of wisdom might just as easily have been invented along the Underground Railroad. There, even the best-laid plans could go awry at a moment's notice. One day it might be severe weather mucking things up. The next, it might be the sound of bloodhounds, or the appearance of a reward poster. The day after that, who knows—a broken-down wagon, a leaky boat, or a chance encounter with the wrong person?

Conductors and station masters had to be fast on their feet. The flexibility and creativity they brought to moments of crisis often made the difference between freedom and failure for fugitives. Harriet Tubman excelled in dicey moments—she could improvise with the best of them, and her skills in that regard come into play in this story of an escape in which she played the role of Cupid, reuniting a couple who had been kept apart for seven long years.

STORY
Sailing *South* to Freedom

The lovesick man who approached Harriet Tubman at some point during 1856 remains unnamed in historical records. An escaped slave from Baltimore, he told Tubman the story of how he had been betrothed to a girl named Tilly and how he had to leave her and run away to freedom after hearing rumors that his owner was going to sell him off.

Seven years had passed since he made that escape. Now, he was hearing through the Underground Railroad grapevine that Tilly's master was about to marry her off to someone else. Worried that he would lose her forever, this man hired Tubman to go get Tilly in Baltimore and bring her to him up in the North.

He gave Harriet the money he had been putting aside in some sort of "Free Tilly" fund. It's not clear to me from my reading how often Tubman hired out her services as a conductor, or how those arrangements worked, exactly. But in his account of this particular affair, Tubman's friend Thomas Garrett puts the transaction as plain as can be: "He gave Harriet money, and Tubman made her way to Philadelphia." (She would make her way to Baltimore from there.)

The possibilities are endless. It may be that Tubman guesstimated the costs involved in an operation and asked clients to cover the cost of keeping runaways in food, shelter, disguises, and other essentials. With bounty hunters and police in pursuit, they might also need forged passes, train tickets, ferry rides, and who knows what else—often on a moment's notice.

It's also possible that Tubman charged rates that would generate a profit after expenses, something that some other conductors were known to do. Later in life, Tubman would demonstrate a strong entrepreneurial streak, starting up several different small businesses in upstate New York. Perhaps she sometimes applied a small-business mindset to her work on the Underground Railroad, generating profits that could then be applied to support future missions and finance rescues of her own family members.

Harriet arrived in Baltimore that October. She managed to locate Tilly despite the fact that the girl was in hiding from her master. There is no telling what plan Harriet had in mind originally for this "young and pretty mulatto." Tubman biographer Sarah Bradford makes mention of a steamboat that she had planned on boarding being "disabled" and unavailable. Perhaps that boat had a friendly, familiar face among the crew that Harriet knew she could count on.

She had arrived in Baltimore with a letter signed by another such friendly face, a steamboat captain in Philadelphia. This note offered assurances that Harriet was a free resident of that city. She had no such note for Tilly, however.

In order to transport a black woman without proper paperwork into a northern port, steamships required a steep cash bond. Harriet didn't have the money for that bond. Instead, she and Tilly ran a misdirection play, by heading south instead of north. They boarded the steamboat *Kent* at Dugan's Wharf in Baltimore. (That wharf was located in the midst of today's touristy Inner Harbor, near the Marine Mammal Pavilion of the National Aquarium.)

The trip aboard that vessel started with a harrowing moment. Here is Bradford again:

> They joined the stream of people going up to get their tickets, but when Harriet asked for hers, the clerk eyed her suspiciously, and said: "You just stand aside, you two; I'll attend to your case bye and bye."
>
> Harriet led the young girl to the bow of the boat, where they were alone, and here, having no other help, she, as was her custom, addressed herself to the Lord.
>
> Kneeling on the seat, and supporting her head on her hands, and fixing her eyes on the waters of the bay, she groaned:
>
> "Oh, Lord! You've been wid me in six troubles, don't desert me in the seventh!" [This is likely a reference to the fact that this was Tubman's seventh rescue mission.]
>
> "Moses! Moses!" cried Tilly, pulling her by the sleeve. "Do go and see if you can't get tickets now."
>
> "Oh, Lord! You've been wid me in six troubles, don't desert me in the seventh."

And so Harriet's story goes on in her peculiarly graphic manner, till at length in terror Tilly exclaimed: "Oh, Moses! the man is coming. What shall we do?"

"Oh, Lord, you've been wid me in six troubles!"

Here the clerk touched her on the shoulder, and Tilly thought their time had come, but all he said was: "You can come now and get your tickets," and their troubles were over.

That boat was headed down the Chesapeake Bay to the mouth of the Nanticoke River, a good way below the Choptank River and the landscape where Harriet had been born and raised. As far as historians can tell, this would be the farthest south that Tubman ever reached in her work on the Underground Railroad. Then the *Kent* turned upriver and made its way up into Delaware, docking in the town of Seaford.

Along the way, Tubman had somehow managed to convince the captain of this steamboat to write a new letter saying that both she *and* Tilly were free residents of Philadelphia. One theory here is that perhaps this captain trusted Tubman's word because he knew and trusted the captain who had provided Tubman with that first letter. Another possibility is that he was sympathetic to the cause of runaways. Who knows? Perhaps it was a combination. Whatever the case, that letter would soon come in handy.

When Tubman and Tilly disembarked in Seaford, they most likely did so at the location of the modern-day Riverwalk on the banks of the Nanticoke River just southeast of the Market Street bridge in the downtown area. As of this writing in 2017, there was quite a lot of construction going on along Seaford's waterfront. A condominium complex was going up on the other side of that bridge. Storefront banners nearby were touting new retail and office spaces as coming soon.

From that Riverwalk spot, Tubman and Tilly walked uphill to the Coulbourn Hotel, which stood on the site of today's Gateway Park, a triangular bit of green space bordered by Market, High, and Front streets. There are benches there, and a pretty fountain. There is also a marker commemorating the day that Tubman and Tilly came through town.

The main commercial corridor in downtown Seaford runs along High Street, to the west. Restaurants and shops lie in that direction, along with the Seaford Museum, which is housed in an expansive old post office and features lots of interesting exhibit materials, including one section related to the story of Tilly and Tubman.

That story picks up again back at the Coulbourn Hotel, where Tubman seems to have taken the full-of-bluster-show-no-fear approach to her situation. As Thomas Garrett describes it, "she boldly went [into] the hotel and called for supper and lodging."

The next morning, on their way out of the hotel, a slave catcher accosted Tubman and Tilly and demanded to know their legal status. Tubman showed off that letter saying she and Tilly were free. The innkeeper apparently intervened here, too, telling the slave catchers to leave his paying guests alone.

From Seaford, Tubman and Tilly probably walked 10 or so miles north to Bridgeville. From there, they boarded a train to Camden, where they hired a carriage to take them to Wilmington. They eventually arrived at the home of Tubman's friend, Thomas Garrett, who soon afterward wrote a letter to a friend dubbing this escape a particularly "remarkable" affair that had "manifested great shrewdness" on the part of Tubman.

[T]he strangest thing about this woman is, she does not know or appears not to know that she has done anything worth notice. May her Guardian continue to preserve her many perilous adventures.

There are countless other examples of Tubman employing creative tricks while conducting her charges to freedom. She would give sedatives to young children to keep them quiet. She would hide slaves in cramped underground potato holes. She would use songs to convey coded messages.

Once when she was back on her home turf of the Eastern Shore, disguised in a bonnet and carting along two chickens as if on a routine errand, she encountered a man described by a biographer as a "former master" (it's not clear who this might have been). She let those chickens loose, making off like it was an accident, and "all of the bystanders roared with laughter as she chased after them." That man never recognized her amid the hubbub.

There is another story—whether legend or truth, it's hard to tell—of a day when Tubman was on a train and saw a white passenger who might recognize her. She picked up a newspaper or book of some sort and pretended to read, even though she was illiterate. That man knew she couldn't read, Tubman explained later. She was simply trying to throw him off, and it worked.

All of these tricks and more put Tubman in a position later in life to make her famous boast that "I never ran my train off the track and I never lost a passenger." That boast was well-earned, of course, but Tubman was also the sort of person who was quick to thank her "Guardian" for helping her through all of those close calls. Here, again, is Bradford, quoting Tubman herself:

> I tell you, Missus, 'twan't me, 'twas de Lord! Jes' so long as he wanted to use me, he would take keer of me.... I always tole him, I'm gwine to hole stiddy onto you, an' you've got to see me trou.

POSTSCRIPT
On Conductors Getting Paid

As chairman of the Vigilance Committee of the Pennsylvania Anti-Slavery Society, William Still served as a primary gatekeeper welcoming runaway slaves as they crossed the border into Pennsylvania and sought help making it on to points north and across to Canada.

Still kept a detailed "Record of Facts, Authentic Narrative, Letters, &C." that he published in 1871 under the title, *The Underground Railroad*. Here is what he had to say on questions that arose surrounding one conductor who charged fees for his services.

[A] captain by the name of B., who owned a schooner, and would bring any kind of freight that would pay the most, was the conductor in this instance. Quite a number of passengers at different times availed themselves of his accommodations and thus succeeded in reaching Canada.

His risk was very great. On this account he claimed, as did certain others, that it was no more than fair to charge for his services—indeed he did not profess to bring persons for nothing, except in rare instances.

In this matter the Committee did not feel disposed to interfere directly in any way, further than to suggest that whatever understanding was agreed upon by the parties themselves should be faithfully adhered to. Many slaves in cities could raise, "by hook or by crook," fifty or one hundred dollars to pay for a passage, providing they could find one who was willing to risk aiding them. Thus, while the Vigilance Committee of Philadelphia ... neither charged nor accepted anything for their services, it was not to be expected that any of the Southern agents could afford to do likewise.

CONNECTIONS

- The "Captain B" that Still mentions in the Postscript above was William Baylis. His work on the Underground Railroad is featured in Chapter 27.

TRAVEL RESOURCES

In addition to its Tubman materials, the **Seaford Museum** has a display about the notorious slave kidnapper and murderer Patty Cannon. Check with the museum in advance for current seasonal hours before visiting.

- 203 High Street, Seaford, Delaware
- SeafordHistoricalSociety.org;
  Facebook.com/SeafordDEHistory; 302.628.9828

Information about things to do and places to go in and around Seaford is available from **Southern Delaware Tourism**.

- VisitSouthernDelaware.com;
  Facebook.com/SouthernDelawareTourism;
  800.357.1818

The **Harriet Tubman Underground Railroad Byway** runs through both Dorchester and Caroline counties in Maryland and then on into Delaware.

- Maryland: HarrietTubmanByway.org; Facebook.com/HarrietTubmanByway; 410.228.1000
- Delaware: TubmanBywayDelaware.org

13: Sidelight: The View Down Below

Seaford, Delaware

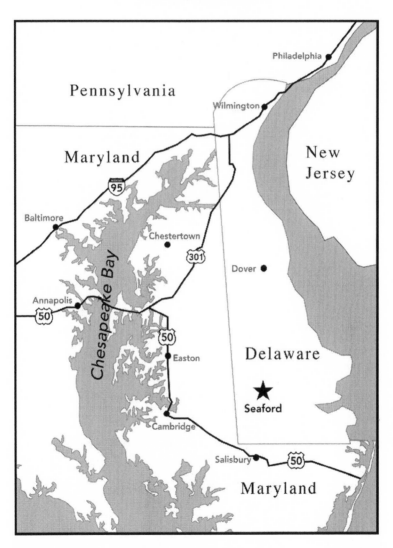

Here is a mystery worth pondering while still in Seaford, Delaware: What about the lower part of the Delmarva Peninsula?

The steamboat voyage that Harriet Tubman took with that girl named Tilly in the previous chapter involved sailing down the Chesapeake Bay to the Nanticoke River and then turning back up toward Seaford. The mouth of the Nanticoke was the southernmost point Tubman reached while working on the Underground Railroad.

We will not be traveling farther south in this book, either, and the question is: How could that be? The journey from here in Seaford down to the southernmost tip of the Eastern Shore at Cape Charles, Virginia covers 120 miles of a landscape that was just full of slaves in Tubman's time as the upper part of the peninsula.

Plenty of slaves ran away down there. In researching his book, *Slave and Free on Virginia's Eastern Shore*, the writer Kirk Mariner found numerous mentions of escapes in court and newspaper records. For whatever reason, however, those slaves almost never found their way to the office of Underground Railroad chronicler William Still in Philadelphia, or to some other sympathetic person who might record their stories.

There are only two mentions of the Eastern Shore of Virginia in Still's records. Both cases involved runaways who found their way to him on their own, without getting help from established conductors or station masters. Did the Underground Railroad even operate on the lower peninsula? It's not really clear at this point. Perhaps some researcher in the years to come find the records that provide a fuller answer. For now, we will have to settle for small snippets.

- In a difficult-to-follow 40-page narrative, a slave named Solomon Bayley writes about a flight from bondage that takes him from Richmond up to Delaware and includes stops at a couple of recognizable locations on the Virginia end of the peninsula, Nandew (presumably Nandua) and Hunting Creek (west of Parksley).

- In August 1829, an armed group of slaves stole a boat and set up camp on an island off of Accomack County, Virginia. This led nearby slave owners to petition the governor for a supply of arms that might help keep such rebellious slaves in check.

- The story William Still tells about a runaway named Peter Matthews of Temperanceville, Virginia contains an intriguing snippet. Matthews said he didn't have enough money to hire a conductor, so perhaps the Underground Railroad was functioning down that way after all.

The remarkable case of Henry Jarvis is perhaps the best demonstration that the stories that unfolded down below on the peninsula—most of them still undiscovered, or perhaps lost forever—are likely every bit as memorable as the ones in this book. Jarvis ran away from Northampton County, Virginia during the early part of the Civil War, fleeing a master who ranked as

> de meanest man on all de Easter's sho' [of Virginia], and dat's a heap to say. It's a rough place. ... Dey don't think so much of their niggers as dey do ob deir dogs. D'rather whip one dan eat any day.

When that master took a shot at Jarvis one day for no apparent reason, Jarvis took off, leaving a wife behind. He stole a canoe and made his way across a wide expanse of open water to the Union Army outpost near Norfolk, where he tried to enlist, only to be told "it warn't a black man's war." (Black soldiers were not welcomed into the Union Army early on in the conflict.)

Instead, Jarvis found work on ships that took him first to Cuba and then to Africa. He returned to the United States in 1863, landing in Boston. By that time, the war had turned into a "black man's war" after all. He tried to enlist in the famed 54th Massachusetts Regiment, but it was full up. He ended up instead in the 55th. He was wounded three times in a battle down in South Carolina. He eventually lost a leg as a result of those wounds.

In an interview conducted long after the war, Jarvis recounted how he had gotten in touch with the wife he had left behind in slavery.

I sent for her, and she sent me word that she thought she'd marry another man. After the war was ober, ... she sen's me word her husban' is dead, but I tol' her she [might] a kep me when she had me, 'n I could get one I liked better, 'n so I have.

That same interviewer asked Jarvis if he had managed to forgive his former master.

Es suh! I'se forgub him; de Lord knows I'se forgub him!

He did, however, want to add one last thought on that topic:

But I'd gib my oder leg to meet him in battle!

TESTIMONY

Like Henry Jarvis in the story above, James Massey left a wife behind when he ran away from slavery in Queen Anne's County, Maryland. He and Henrietta had been married less than a year. Upon reaching Canada, James sent a letter to William Still at the Anti-Slavery Society in Philadelphia and asked that the following message be forwarded to Henrietta.

Dear Wife,

I take this opertunity to inform you that I have Arive in [Canada] this Eving, After Jorney of too weeks, and now find mysilf on free ground and wish that you was here with me.

But you are not here. When we parted I did not know that I should come away so soon as I did. But for that of causin you pain [because] I left as I did, I hope that you will try to come. But if you cannot, write to me as soon as you can and tell me all that you can.

But don't be Desscuredged. I was sory to leave you. ... You must not think that I did not care for you. I cannot tell how I come, for I was some times on the earth and some times under the earth.

Do not Bee afraid to come, but start and keep trying, if you are afrid fitch your ... sister with you for compeny, and I will take care of you and treat you like a lady so long as you live.

The talk of cold in this place is all a humbug, it is wormer here than it was there when I left. Your father and mother has allways treated me like their own child. I have no fault to find in them. I send my Respects to them Both, and I hope that they will remember me in Prayer.

Tell [my] father and mother that I am safe and hope that they will not morn after me. I shall ever Remember them. No more at present. But yours in Body and mind, and if we no meet on Earth I hope that we shall meet in heven.

Your husbern. Good night.
Jame[s] Masey

Alas, when Still published this letter many years later, he reported that Underground Railroad agents never found a way to deliver James's letter, so it seems that Henrietta never got a chance to read what her husband had to say. I do not know if the two ever saw each other again.

14: A Mother's Love Is a Mysterious Thing (Christmas Escape, Part 3)

Choptank, Maryland

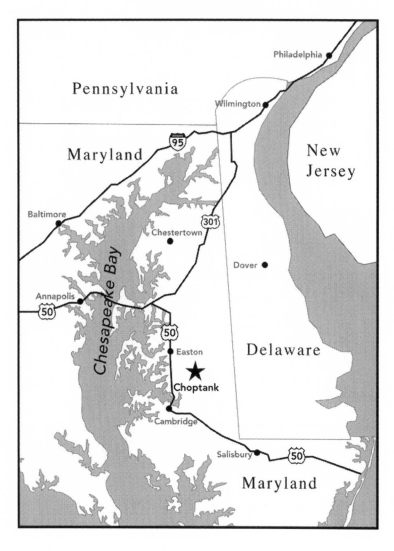

BIG PICTURE
Family First

No one knows the exact location of the cabin where Rit and Ben Ross, the parents of Harriet Tubman, lived from the late 1840s through the mid-1850s, except to say that it was in the area of Maryland's Eastern Shore known then and now as Poplar Neck. The nearby town of Choptank is the place to go and think about what a big role that little cabin played in the life of Harriet Tubman.

It's fitting that Tubman relied so heavily on the home of her parents in her work as a conductor. There were a good number of strangers and vague acquaintances among the seventy or so slaves she led to freedom, but they were not the primary reason Tubman signed on to work along the Underground Railroad in the first place.

First and foremost, she was in it for family. She told her biographer, Sarah Bradford, that the jubilation she felt after her own escape was tempered by a bittersweet aspect of homesickness.

> I had crossed de line of which I had so long been dreaming. I was free, but dere was no one to welcome me to de land of freedom. I was a stranger in a strange land, and my home after all was down [in Maryland] wid de ole folks, and my brudders and sisters.

There are many things about Tubman's life that remain mysterious today, but the source of her extraordinary devotion to family is not one of them. Later in life, Tubman told a story about her mother from the days when Tubman and her siblings were still young—the family was living below Cambridge, Maryland at the time.

A slave trader from Georgia showed up one day and cut a deal with Rit's owner, Edward Brodess, to buy a boy named Moses. Moses was Rit's youngest son, and Tubman's little brother. Rit grew suspicious about this situation straight away. After catching a glimpse of Brodess counting up some money and then ordering one of his other slaves to go and fetch Moses, she leaped into action.

Darn if that boy didn't all of a sudden go "missing," and then stay that way for perhaps a month. Moses would sleep in the woods one night, with a friend the next, and who knows where on the one after that. A network of family and friends helped Rit get messages to the boy and deliver his meals.

Eventually, however, one of those helpers betrayed the game, telling Brodess where he could find the boy. But even then, Rit managed to stay a step ahead of the white men. When Brodess and that slave trader appeared at the spot where their source had told them they would find Moses, there was no sign of the boy.

The men decided to pay a call at Rit's cabin in an effort to resolve the situation.

"What do you want?" Rit asked them.

"Mr. Scott wants to come in and light a segar," Brodess answered.

Rit "ripped out an oath" and then said, "You are after my son; but the first man comes into my house, I will split his head open."

Brodess eventually backed down and canceled the sale of Moses.

That story makes it easy to see where Tubman came by her intense devotion to family, doesn't it? And it probably goes a long way toward explaining where she came by her uncommon reserves of courage, too.

STORY
A Mother's Love Is a Mysterious Thing

Yes, a mother's love can fill a heart with the kind of courage that Rit showed when she feared losing her son to a slave trader. But it can also be a source of weakness—or at least that was the thinking of Tubman, her father, and three of her brothers during the Christmas Escape.

This was, arguably, the most eventful undertaking of Tubman's career as a conductor. The advance preparations for the December 1854 rendezvous that is the focus of this story were complex, emotionally wrenching affairs that are detailed in two other chapters of this book.

This third part of the story picks up here, at Poplar Neck. The drive back into Maryland from our previous stop in Seaford, Delaware is a two-lane affair dominated by farmland and dotted with small stands of trees. Poplar Neck is just below the town Preston, at the point where Choptank Road ends in a town of the same name.

There are no shops or amenities here—fewer than 100 people call it home—but you will find a postcard-pretty marina and a sweeping view of the river. The marina has a couple of markers that commemorate the importance of nearby Poplar Neck during Underground Railroad times. If you are looking at the river, Poplar Neck is to the north, upriver on your right-hand side. The cabin where Ben and Rit lived was most likely a one-room affair built of logs hand-hewn by Ben with a little help from friends. Its little loft would have been accessible by ladder rather than stairs.

A free man at this point, Ben was working during his Poplar Neck years in the timbering operations of Dr. Anthony C. Thompson, the son of his former owner. Thompson owned some 2,000 acres hereabouts.

Harriet Tubman probably stopped here during her own run to freedom in 1849. She likely used her parents' cabin as a station during at least three other escapes as well. Other slaves made their way north with Ben's help, too—it's impossible to say how many.

This whole area was a hotbed of Underground Railroad activity. Another station master, the free black Rev. Samuel Green, lived five or so miles away in East New Market. A third station was located just up the road near Preston in the home of a white Quaker family, the Levertons. (That home is still standing along

Seaman Road, but it's privately owned and not accessible to the public.)

The scene to imagine on Poplar Neck is Christmas Eve, 1854. Robert Ross was probably the last of Harriet's three brothers to arrive, after somehow managing to tear himself away from his wife and newborn child to join in the escape attempt. Along with Ben and Henry Ross, he was running under a frightful deadline, as all three brothers were slated to go up on the slave auction block the day after Christmas.

Rit must have been going about her preparations for Christmas dinner that day with quite the mix of anticipation and trepidation. How long had it been since she last saw her sons? Those sons were enslaved, after all, and lived some 25 miles away. Opportunities for family reunions in those circumstances must have been few and far between.

Then there was the matter of that auction looming ahead. Perhaps a local buyer would scoop the brothers up, allowing them to stay in the area. But perhaps not: Years earlier, three of Rit's daughters had been sold to out-of-state owners and shipped into the Deep South, never to be seen again.

Would this Christmas dinner be the last time she saw these three sons?

This is where that business about a mother's love comes in. Ben Ross and his four adult children made a decision that day to keep Rit in the dark about the escape that was in the works. Years later, they talked about this decision by describing how they were worried that Rit would not be able to keep her emotions in check. They thought she might raise such an all-out ruckus of grief over this unexpected farewell that it would draw unwanted attention to the cabin.

Tubman and the brothers hid from her in a little outbuilding that served as a corncrib. There, they watched through a crack in the door while their mother prepared the Christmas dinner they would not be sitting down to eat.

Perhaps Ben, Tubman, and the brothers were worried, too, about whether Rit would hold up under questioning once the brothers' owner alerted local authorities that Robert, Ben, and Henry had gone missing.

After all, Ben was worried about his own ability to deal with those questions. He put on a blindfold that Christmas Eve every time he came near Harriet and the brothers. When it came time for them to start making their way to the next station, he walked blindly with them for a bit, removing the covering from his eyes only after they were all out of sight.

Those investigators did show up asking their questions soon enough. And in response, Ben told them the truth: He hadn't *seen* his sons at all around Christmastime.

In the books and essays about Tubman that I've read, this story is presented as a triumphant tale. It does have a happy ending, after all—the brothers all made it north to Canada in the end. Ben's cleverness with that blindfold business is something to celebrate as well.

But then there is Rit, and she is why this story always leaves me with a nagging bit of sadness. It leaves me imagining the way she toiled away on that Christmas dinner, so full of anticipation over the coming gift of time together with three sons who would soon be headed up on the auction block.

Then those sons failed to show up. And then there are Ben and Rit, eating that holiday dinner alone. I imagine that Ben is feeling a need to keep lying to his wife by saying he has no idea what's up with Ben, Robert, and Henry. And I imagine that Rit's heart is breaking a little bit more with each passing minute of Christmas Day.

TESTIMONY
'Go,' Said I, 'and Break Your Mother's Heart.'

In her autobiographical narrative, *Incidents in the Life of a Slave Girl*, Harriet Jacobs recounts a goodbye moment in her North Carolina family that is the sort of encounter that the Ross brothers decided to avoid with their mother during the Christmas Escape. Here, an uncle of Jacobs is breaking the news to her that he is going to make a run for it. (Jacobs wrote her book using a pseudonym, Linda Brent, which is why she is referring to herself here by that name.)

"I have come," said Benjamin, "to tell you good by. I am going away."

I inquired where.

"To the north," he replied.

I looked at him to see whether he was in earnest. I saw it all in his firm, set mouth. I implored him not to go, but he paid no heed to my words. He said he was no longer a boy, and every day made his yoke more galling. He had raised his hand against his master, and was to be publicly whipped for the offence.

I reminded him of the poverty and hardships he must encounter among strangers. I told him he might be caught and brought back; and that was terrible to think of. He grew vexed, and asked if poverty and hardships with freedom, were not preferable to our treatment in slavery.

"Linda," he continued, "we are dogs here; footballs, cattle, every thing that's mean. No, I will not stay. Let them bring me back. We don't die but once."

He was right; but it was hard to give him up.

"Go," said I, "and break your mother's heart."

I repented of my words ere they were out.

"Linda," said he, speaking as I had not heard him speak that evening, "how could you say that? Poor mother! be kind to her, Linda."

... Farewells were exchanged, and the bright, kind boy, endeared to us by so many acts of love, vanished from our sight. How vividly does memory bring back that sad night!

Benjamin was captured and brought back to North Carolina on that escape attempt, but he eventually made it to freedom.

CONNECTIONS

- The first part of the Christmas Escape is in Chapter 5. The second part is in Chapter 7.
- The story of Rev. Samuel Green, one of the other conductors mentioned here, is in Chapter 11.
- Tubman would return to Poplar Neck several years after the Christmas Escape to bring her parents north to Canada. That story is in Chapter 15.

TRAVEL RESOURCES

Gas, food, and other amenities are available in **Preston**, Maryland just a few miles up the road from Choptank. Choptank is unincorporated, so the official address below for the marina there has it in Preston.

- 21843 Water Street, Preston, Maryland

We have crossed into Caroline County, Maryland here. Information about things to do and places to go nearby is available from **Caroline County Tourism**.

- Caroline Visitor Center, 5 Crouse Park Lane,
  Denton, Maryland
- TourCaroline.com;
  Facebook.com/CarolineTourism; 410.479.0655

The **Harriet Tubman Underground Railroad Byway** runs through both Dorchester and Caroline counties in Maryland and then on into Delaware.

- Maryland: HarrietTubmanByway.org;
  Facebook.com/HarrietTubmanByway;
  410.228.1000
- Delaware: TubmanBywayDelaware.org

15: Saving Mom and Dad

Choptank, Maryland

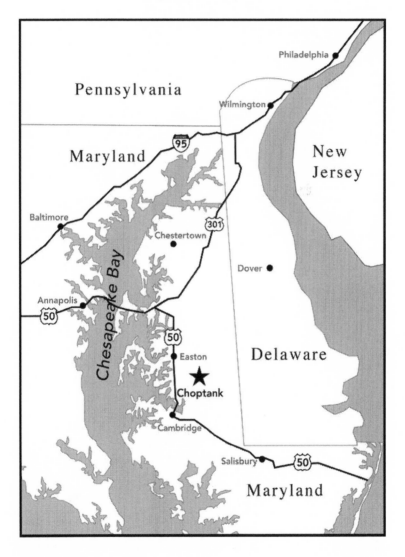

BIG PICTURE
Senior Moments

Several stories elsewhere in this book speak to just how fierce a sense of family loyalty took hold early on in the heart of Araminta Ross, long before she grew up and turned herself into Harriet Tubman.

Such devotion is bound to hit some bumps along the road of life. How, for example, do you respond when your brothers let you down, as Tubman's did when they bailed out on her first escape attempt? She responded to that disappointment by coming back to rescue those same brothers several years later.

Consider, too, the task of caring for our elders. By all accounts, Tubman's mother, Rit Ross, grew into quite a cantankerous woman in her older years, serving up a constant litany of complaints and recriminations. Here is how Tubman biographer Sarah Bradford describes the elderly Rit's state of mind:

> [She was] querulous and exacting and most unreasonable in her temper, often reproaching this faithful daughter as the Israelites did of Moses of old, for "bringing them up in the wilderness to die there of hunger."

Tubman's father, Ben Ross, was a working man through and through. He spent his youth and middle age toiling day in and day out as a timbering supervisor. There isn't much information available about his emotional state in his older years, but it seems fair to assume that the physical challenges he encountered due to a bad case of arthritis boiled over now and again into flashes of anger and frustration.

This book focuses on the Underground Railroad years and is set on the Delmarva Peninsula, so there is not much here about Tubman's life after the Civil War, when she lived in the town of Auburn, in upstate New York. In many ways, however, the stories from the last half of this woman's life are just as interesting and compelling as the ones from her younger years.

Tubman remained as devoted as ever to family in her later years. First and foremost, that devotion manifested itself in caring for her parents. Over time, that experience inspired her to take on a new mission, the creation of a then-groundbreaking kind of facility where elders in the black community might spend their last days in a safe and comforting atmosphere.

The way I think about this part of Tubman's journey, it likely began back in the chilly spring of 1857, when she set out from the North to return to her parents' cabin on Poplar Neck and help them out of a bad spot.

STORY
Saving Mom and Dad

The law would be coming after Ben Ross next. A sensational, highly publicized escape by the so-called Dover Eight in March of 1857 was the last straw for slave owners on Maryland's Eastern Shore. Furious and embarrassed, they demanded that local authorities tear up the Underground Railroad once and for all.

The first station master to fall was Rev. Samuel Green of East New Market. Arrested in early April, he would soon be sentenced to 10 years in prison for the crime of having a copy of *Uncle Tom's Cabin*.

Like Green, Ben Ross had probably given safe harbor to the Dover Eight on their run to freedom. He was likely involved in many other escapes as well, including a recent one that may have aggravated the trouble he was in that spring. Tubman biographer Sarah Bradford says that right around this time,

> the old man had been betrayed by a slave whom he had assisted, but who had turned back [and returned to his or her master].

If Ben had any doubts about whether he, too, was going to get caught up in the legal crackdown on Underground Railroad activity, those doubts were erased when his "master" tipped him off to the fact that his arrest was imminent. That master also advised him to leave the state, pronto.

Ben and Rit were both legally free by this point. They didn't have masters. Most likely, this confusing reference in the historical record is intended to mean Dr. Anthony C. Thompson, the son of the master who had owned Ben for most of his life in slavery. Ben did a lot of paid work for this younger Thompson, who owned thousands of acres of forestland on and around Poplar Neck.

Another possibility is that the tip came from John Stewart. Ben had been hired out by his former master to work in Stewart's forestry operations over a good number of his younger years. There has been some speculation among historians that Stewart may have become a sort of "surrogate master" to Ben.

Either way, it's interesting that a powerful white man would make the effort to give Ben such a heads-up. Was that tip driven by a genuine affection built up over Ben's many years of service? Or was it a more selfish affair, linked perhaps to a fear of public embarrassment if one of "their blacks" were to get caught up in a well-publicized arrest?

After hearing about her parents' troubles through the Underground Railroad grapevine, Tubman encountered a terrible string of complications making her way down from Canada that spring. She had no money, for starters. She stopped in Syracuse to ask for support from a white abolitionist, but he turned her down. She stopped in New York City, too, and managed to cobble together a few dollars during a visit to the office of that city's branch of the Anti-Slavery Society. A run of wicked storms and cold temperatures on the Eastern Seaboard added to her delays.

She finally arrived in late May, at which point she learned that Ben was due in court in just a few short days. In one of the many memorable turns of phrase that this illiterate woman came up with in her long life, this is how she summed up the mission at hand:

> I just removed my father's trial to a higher court, and brought him off to Canada.

Her parents were both approaching 70 years old by this point. They couldn't very well walk the Underground Railroad route in the manner of most of Tubman's previous passengers. Tubman had managed to get a hold of a pathetic old horse, and she had cobbled together an amateurish "carriage" that was little more than a flat board propped atop an old axle and wheels. She rigged up makeshift stirrups so that Rit and Ben would be able to rest their feet while sitting on that board.

Many people who have pitched in to help an aging parent will be able to relate to what happened when Tubman finally arrived at Poplar Neck and told her parents that they needed to move, quickly. They dawdled instead. Ben argued that he needed to bring along his cherished timbering tools. Rit announced that she wasn't leaving without her precious feather bed.

The rig had no space for such items, so it became Tubman's turn to play the role of parent. She ordered Ben and Rit to climb aboard, and off they went, north from Poplar Neck and on into Delaware on a carriage ride of forty-some miles. Between the cold weather, the lack of creature comforts, and the tragic absence of her feather bed, Rit was probably complaining the whole way.

They crossed into Delaware and reached the town of Camden, near Dover. There, Tubman escorted her parents onto a train bound for Wilmington. Then she went back out to that carriage, riding in peaceful solitude for another 50 or so miles before meeting up with them again. The trio spent a night at the Wilmington home of station master Thomas Garrett before continuing on to Philadelphia and the Anti-Slavery Society office there run by William Still.

Still's account of his interview with Tubman's parents is full of inexplicable oddities. He says that Ben and Rit were still slaves, when in fact they were both legally free at this point. Did Tubman and her parents lie about their status? Or, perhaps, did Still have to fudge things in the official record in order to make any assistance he gave to this party fit into the rules of his organization?

Ben went on a bit of a tirade during this interview. He described Dr. Thompson, the son of his former owner, as a "wolf in sheep's clothing" and as a "spare-built man, bald head, wearing a wig." He made fun of the younger Thompson's status as a minister, saying that the man had been "pretending to preach for 20 years."

Ben also complained about the sale of three of his daughters into the Deep South many years before, but this was something that neither Thompson nor Thompson's father had any involvement with. Those daughters had been sold by Rit's previous owners—that was another family altogether, the Brodesses.

Again, this might have all been a clever bit of play-acting for the official records of the Anti-Slavery Society. But perhaps not: Could it be that Ben's memory was starting to go a bit south? Were the various indignities and heartaches he had suffered in slavery getting jumbled up in his mind and pouring out in ways that didn't quite make sense? This is nothing but speculation on my part, but it comes naturally here in an age when we all know families dealing with issues of dementia.

After arriving in Canada, Ben and Rit enjoyed plenty of happy moments, seeing their long-lost sons and meeting a few new grandchildren. Such family joys aside, however, Rit despised life in St. Catharine's, Ontario. It was much too cold for her tastes. She had lots of other complaints, too:

> The old mother had no tobacco and no tea—and these were more essential to her comfort than food or clothing; then reproaches thick and fast fell upon Harriet.

One winter in Canada was all Rit could handle. Tubman set about finding a new home for her parents before the following winter, which is how she ended up in upstate New York and started on that journey to establish the Harriet Tubman Home for the Aged.

TESTIMONY
'I'm Gwine Home to Tell Lawd Jesus All About It'

Tubman's journey toward building that old people's home in Auburn, New York was a long and winding affair. One key moment along the way came when a 25-acre parcel of land right near her home came up for auction. As always, Tubman was short of funds at this moment. Her recurring financial troubles were apparently common knowledge among her neighbors. But she showed up for that auction anyway, and here is the account she gave Sarah Bradford of what happened next:

> Dey was all white folks but me dere, Missus, and dere I was like a blackberry in a pail [of] milk, but I hid down in a corner, and no one know'd who was biddin'.
>
> De man began [the bidding] down pretty low, and I kept goin' up by fifties; he got up to twelve hundred, thirteen hundred, fourteen hundred, and still dat voice in the corner kept goin' up by fifties.
>
> At last it got up to fourteen hundred and fifty, an' den oders stopped biddin', an' de man said, "All done! who is de buyer?"
>
> "Harriet Tubman," I shouted.
>
> "What! dat ole nigger?" dey said. "Old woman, how you ebber gwine to pay fer dat lot [of] land?"

"I'm gwine home to tell de Lawd Jesus all about it," I said.

That talk with Jesus did the trick, apparently. Tubman managed eventually to pay for that land and build the old people's home, though it took many years and involved mortgaging just about everything she had and bringing in a local church as a partner. The Harriet Tubman Home for the Aged opened at last on June 23, 1908.

Tubman herself moved into the facility when she was no longer healthy enough to stay in her own home. She died there in her early 90s, on March 10, 1913.

CONNECTIONS

- In the Testimony section of Chapter 10, there is a full account of the very interesting fundraising stop that Tubman made at the Anti-Slavery Society office in New York City.
- The roots of Tubman's devotion to her mother and her family are touched on in the stories in Chapter 4 and Chapter 14.
- The story of the Dover Eight is told in full in Chapter 29.
- The story of Ben Ross's neighbor, Rev. Samuel Green, is in Chapter 11.

TRAVEL RESOURCES

This chapter is set in the same location as the previous one, in the town of Choptank. Gas, food, and other amenities are available in **Preston**, Maryland just a few miles up the road. Choptank is unincorporated, so the official address below for the town's marina has it in Preston.

- 21843 Water Street, Preston, Maryland

Information about things to do and places to go in Caroline County is available from **Caroline County Tourism**.

- Caroline Visitor Center, 5 Crouse Park Lane, Denton, Maryland
- TourCaroline.com; Facebook.com/CarolineTourism; 410.479.0655

The **Harriet Tubman Underground Railroad Byway** runs through both Dorchester and Caroline counties in Maryland and then on into Delaware.

- Maryland: HarrietTubmanByway.org; Facebook.com/HarrietTubmanByway; 410.228.1000
- Delaware: TubmanBywayDelaware.org

16: Side Trip: The Webb Cabin

Harmony, Maryland

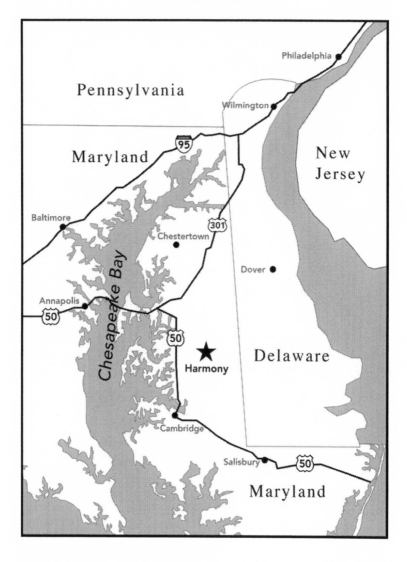

Various little cabins play central roles in the stories of the Underground Railroad in this book. There is the one on Peter's Neck where Harriet Tubman was born; another on Tuckahoe Creek where Frederick Douglass spent his childhood; still another on Poplar Neck where Tubman's parents lived later in life; and several others to boot.

The best place on Maryland's Eastern Shore to get a feel for what those cabins might have been like is the restored James H. Webb Cabin, which is just off of Route 16 between Preston and Harmony, on Grove Road. It was built by a free black man, James Webb, in 1852. He shared the house with his enslaved wife, Mary Ann, their four children—Charles, Elizabeth, John, and Ann; and Webb's father, Henry.

There is no evidence that this particular cabin was used along the Underground Railroad, but it stands as a rare surviving remnant of day-to-day black life back in slavery times. Built with hand-hewn logs set on a foundation of ballast stones from tall ships, which Webb had liberated from nearby rivers, it's a one-room affair with a loft that could be accessed only by ladder. It's probably quite similar to the other cabins mentioned in these pages, including the one Ben Ross built just a few miles away on Poplar Neck, which definitely did serve as a station along the Underground Railroad.

Tours of the Webb cabin are self-guided affairs. You just pull up, park, and wander around the grounds, and then into the house through the back door. Think on your visit about the fact that seven people shared these tight quarters on a daily basis in Webb's time. Be sure, too, to check out the trap door in the floor that leads to a little below-ground compartment used by the Webbs for storing perishable foods. Slaves on the run were known to hide out in "potato holes" like this when bounty hunters and sheriffs were hot on their trail.

Webb eventually bought the freedom of his wife. I am not sure of the status of his children up through the years of the Civil War. Webb lived in the cabin for more than half a century before selling it in 1906. The Caroline County historian J.O.K. Walsh puts Webb's death in the years between 1907 and 1910, which would have put him in his late 80s.

TESTIMONY
Cabin Life

The former slave Fannie Moore was interviewed during the Depression years by writers collecting slave narratives for the Federal Writers' Project. Here, she recalls the day-to-day affairs of life in her family's cabin in Moore, South Carolina. This is from *When I Was a Slave: Memoirs from the Slave Narrative Collection*.

De quarters [were] just [a] long row of cabins daubed with dirt. Everyone in de family live in one big room. In one end was a big fireplace. Dis had to heat de cabin and do de cookin' too. We cooked in a big pot hung on a rod over de fire and bake de corn pone in de ashes, or else put it in de skillet and cover de lid with coals. We always have plenty wood to keep us warm. Dat is if we have time to get it out of de woods.

My granny she cook for us chillens while our mammy away in de field. Dey wasn't much cookin' to do. Just make corn pone and bring in de milk. She have a big wooden bowl with enough wooden spoons to go round. She put de milk in de bowl and break it up. Den she put de bowl in de middle of de floor and all de chillen grab a spoon.

TRAVEL RESOURCES

The **James H. Webb Cabin** is west of Route 16 along Grove Road, which is between Preston on the south and Harmony on the north. As far as I can tell, it does not have a traditional street address attached to it, but if you Google "James H. Webb Cabin," you will find your way to a detailed map easily enough. The property is managed by the Caroline County Historical Society.

- CarolineHistory.org/places/james-h-webb-cabin/; 410.479.2730

The landscape here is mostly rural farmland, where shops and restaurants are few and far between. There are amenities in the nearby town of **Preston**, Maryland. Another option is **Mary's Country Store**, 6244 Harmony Road in Preston. (The store is actually in the tiny town of Harmony, which is unincorporated—that's why the official address is in Preston.)

While in this area, you may want to check out the **William Still Interpretive Center**, located between the Webb Cabin and the site of the next chapter, downtown Denton. As this book was going to press in 2017, the Caroline County Historical Society was working on adding new signage and exhibit panels to the site, as well as opening up public access to the interior of a restored wood-frame cabin there. That cabin is probably quite similar to the one where William Still's parents lived while enslaved here in Caroline County. Both eventually ended up in New Jersey, where Still was born in about 1820. Still grew up to become a leader of the Pennsylvania Anti-Slavery Society and a key chronicler of the events and people of the Underground Railroad.

- Caroline County 4-H Park, 8320 Detour Road, Denton, Maryland
- HarrietTubmanByway.org/william-still-interpretive-center; 410.479.2730

Information about things to do and places to go here in Caroline County is available from **Caroline County Tourism**.

- 5 Crouse Park Lane, Denton, Maryland
- TourCaroline.com; Facebook.com/CarolineTourism; 410.479.0655

The **Harriet Tubman Underground Railroad Byway** runs through both Dorchester and Caroline counties in Maryland and then on into Delaware.

- Maryland: HarrietTubmanByway.org; Facebook.com/HarrietTubmanByway; 410.228.1000
- Delaware: TubmanBywayDelaware.org

17: THE OTHER MOSES

Denton, Maryland

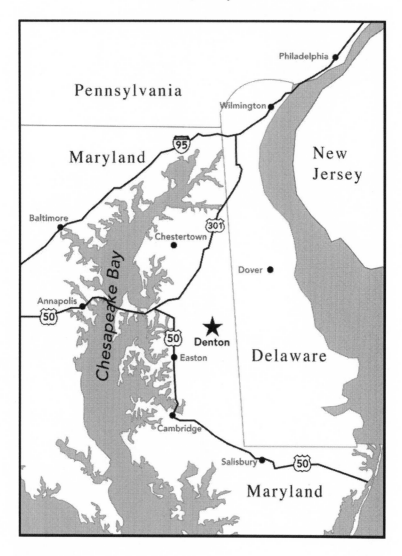

BIG PICTURE
Free or Fugitive?

Over and over in this book, I use phrases like "run to freedom" and "escape from bondage," but they are oversimplifications. Even after reaching free states, former slaves were at risk of getting caught and dragged back into slavery. The way fugitive slaves were treated was the subject of intense national debate dating clear back to 1793, when Congress passed the first Fugitive Slave Act in an attempt to make sure slave owners had access to their "property" even in states where slavery had been outlawed.

The states where anti-slavery sentiment ran strong soon set about devising ways to get around this law, however. One such strategy involved requiring jury trials in fugitive cases. Jurors in those states were often unsympathetic toward slave owners and tended to rule against them, no matter the evidence. A few states went even further, passing laws that forbade local officials from getting involved in fugitive cases at all.

The issue came to a head once again with the passage of a second, more aggressive Fugitive Slave Act in 1850. This law upped the ante of federal control, levying stiff fines against local officials who refused to help slave owners take their "property" back.

The passage of this second law set off a panic among fugitive slaves, especially after some sensationalized media coverage about the first handful of cases where it came into play. A frenzied migration from the northern states soon began, with the escapees moving by the hundreds and then the thousands across the border into Canada. Black neighborhoods in some New England cities nearly emptied out altogether.

Both stories in this chapter touch on this issue. The men at the center of the stories ran from Maryland's Eastern Shore and built successful new lives for themselves in northern college towns, only to find their newfound freedom slipping out of their fingers.

STORY
The Other Moses

Moses Viney had a pretty fun go of it for the first seven years of life. His best childhood pal was a white boy named Richard, and the two of them had the run of a farm in Talbot County, Maryland. The two boys even shared a birthday, March 10, though Richard was a year older, having been born in 1816.

Their friendship cooled once Moses turned seven, however. This seems to be the way things worked during those years in many households on the Eastern Shore. Friendships between black and white children would flourish early on, then fade quickly once they reached the age when black kids went to work as slaves and white children started into schooling on their way to becoming masters in their own right down the road.

Most of the sources I've reviewed place the farm of Richard's father, William Murphy, somewhere in the vicinity of Trappe, a town in southernmost Talbot

County, just across the Choptank River from Cambridge. (A couple other sources place it outside of Easton, the county seat.) The primary crops young Moses helped to plant and harvest in the Murphy fields were tobacco, corn, and wheat. For a while, around the age of 17 or 18, Moses worked as a butler in the main farmhouse.

Moses was in his early 20s in 1840 when his former childhood pal Richard took over the farm after the death of his father. It was a dicey transition. The elder Murphy had amassed quite a bit of debt, and the timing of his passing was awful. Tobacco markets were in a free fall. Even the Lloyds, the richest family in Talbot County, were having troubles. They sold off hundreds of slaves around this time, trying to raise enough cash to make ends meet.

Moses feared that he, too, was headed for the auction block. It's unclear how long he had been thinking about making a run to freedom. Later in life, he recalled being struck as a child by a phrase he heard often from older slaves in the fields as flocks of birds flew overhead during their spring and fall migrations:

The wild geese come from Canada, where all are free.

If Moses had been born in modern times, I suspect he would have been one of those millionaire-next-door types. He was a planner, through and through, a quality that showed up in the way he saved up a little nest egg for the day he would finally get to follow those geese on a journey north. Overseers on the Murphy farm were in the habit of handing out a few pennies every day to reward whichever slave stacked the most sheaves of wheat or excelled in some other bit of manual labor. Moses won these little contests time and again, until he had amassed the sum of $20.

It was Easter Sunday, 1840, when Moses took off. He had two friends with him, and they were hoping that the holiday would buy them a little extra time before their absence was noticed. Alas, things didn't work out that way. When they tried to cross the Choptank River near Denton, just 17 miles into their long journey, the bloodhounds from the Murphy farm caught up with them.

Did I mention that Moses was a planner? He had fully prepared himself for this turn of events. For months back on the farm, he had secretly befriended those dogs with scraps of food and other bits of love and kindness. Now, at this moment of great danger, those dogs turned tail and headed back home when he ordered them to do so.

This inspired bit of on-the-run cleverness is celebrated today in a historical marker at Daniel Crouse Memorial Park on the Choptank River waterfront in Denton. There is a picnic pavilion there, as well as boat launch facilities and the Caroline County Visitor Center.

Denton is Caroline's county seat. The stop here will put you right on the edge of a downtown with an array of shops, galleries, and eateries. History buffs will want to find their way to the Museum of Rural Life. Outdoors lovers will find a couple of state parks nearby, Tuckahoe to the north and Martinak to the south.

Once Moses shooed those dogs away, the trio followed the banks of the Choptank to the north. You can track their likely route by taking Route 313 up into Greensboro, where there are a couple of more places to enjoy the sights and sounds of the river—at the Greensboro Carnival Grounds, off of Sunset Avenue on the way into downtown, and at Christian Park north of town, where the river narrows considerably at the end of a dirt road called Red Bridges.

At some point in their journey, Moses and his companions stole a canoe, only to find that it had no paddle. They ripped posts from a nearby fence and made do with those. By the end of day two, the Monday after Easter, they were approaching Smyrna, Delaware, which was then a fair-sized port town. There, Moses dug into his hard-earned savings and paid for three seats aboard a stagecoach into town.

The historic district in downtown Smyrna today boasts a number of buildings that were standing when Moses and his companions rolled into town. The trio managed somehow to get on board a steamboat headed for Philadelphia. From there it was onto New York City, where they made connections with an Underground Railroad man who gave Moses the names of some contacts in the upstate town of Troy.

In many of the other stories in this book, there is not all that much information available about what happened later in life to slaves who found their way to freedom. There may be a census-record mention or two about how he is working as a barber or she is a housemaid, but that's about it.

The case of Moses Viney is different—his story in the years after his escape is quite well documented. Those contacts he was supposed to make in Troy didn't really work out. Instead, Moses and his friends wandered across the Hudson River to Schenectady, finding work and lodging on a farm there.

Two years later, Moses was hired by Eliphalet Nott, the president of Union College. The two soon became friends as well as colleagues. Moses seems to have filled the role of Jeeves the Butler to Nott's Bertie Wooster, serving as something closer to a trusted executive assistant than simple butler.

Then came the Fugitive Slave Act of 1850. Reading those sensational media reports about former slaves getting sent back into slavery, Moses grew nervous about the fact that Union College had a good number of southern students who might not be happy about his presence on campus. He shared those concerns with President Nott, who advised the former slave to join in the exodus of fugitives and move to Canada.

Once Moses was safe across the border, Nott set out to fix the problem. Through intermediaries, he reached out to Richard Murphy and asked how much it would cost to purchase Viney's freedom. Murphy started the negotiations at $1,900. Nott responded by telling Murphy how happy Moses was in Canada and how it would be absolutely no problem at all for him to stay there for the rest of his life. I have seen two different numbers for the price that Murphy ended up accepting; it was either $250 or $120. Nott soon sent word north to Moses that he was a fully free man at last and could return to Schenectady and return to his work on campus.

A university publication from that time has a colorful account of one of the more unusual tasks on Moses's to-do list. He assisted students as they ventured out on "innocent escapades of the night," escapades that presumably involved lots of alcohol. The next morning, he would wander through dormitories "to arouse the oversleepers in time to make their morning classes or to get them to chapel." Among the young men Moses shepherded through this rite of passage was a future president of the United States, Chester Arthur.

When President Nott died in 1866, Moses Viney received the princely sum of $1,000 from his will. It was during the postwar Reconstruction years that Moses returned to Talbot County, Maryland and paid a call on his former childhood friend, Richard Murphy. By one account, the visit was a perfectly cordial affair, "notwithstanding the fact that [negotiations over the price of Viney's freedom] had impoverished [Murphy] to the extent of sixteen hundred dollars."

Moses was the eldest of an astounding 21 brothers and sisters, so he had a lot of catching up to do back home. He learned that two of his brothers had also escaped slavery. Both had joined the Union Army and died during the Civil War. He met with at least three other brothers in Maryland, and he adopted a four-year-old half-sister named Leila.

Moses's wife, Anna, died in 1885. When Moses retired from work at the college, he bought himself a horse and carriage and hired himself out as a driver. In the 1890s, one local newspaper in Schenectady reported that "the ladies [of the town] consider it quite 'chic' to shop with Moses."

In his later years, his health failing, Moses ended up in Leila's care. He would go out for daily strolls in this period, during which another newspaper account dubbed him "the most noted and picturesque figure on the streets."

He died in 1909 at the age of 92. A portrait of Moses Viney hangs today on campus at Union College. He has been honored in several ceremonies and presentations at the school over the years. In 2016, a college administrator published a novel titled *A Bonded Friendship: Moses and Eliphalet*.

There is one last footnote to the story of this other Moses that I find quite touching. His funeral seems to have been a big affair in Schenectady, with scholars and social bigwigs and students all turning out in force to bid him a loving farewell. In one account of the ceremony in a college publication, a writer added this little detail:

[S]ome colored friends ordered a floral piece for the coffin that spelled out, "*Free.*"

BONUS STORY
A Fugitive Lands in Princeton

As unlikely as it might seem, there was a second slave from Talbot County, Maryland who made a run for freedom and ended up, like Moses Viney, a prominent figure at a top college. Born a slave 1816, James Collins eventually became the property of a young man named Severn Teackle Wallis, who would go on to become a big-time lawyer, a state legislator, and, eventually, provost of the University of Maryland.

One day in 1839, Wallis gave Collins $5 and told him to run an errand. Collins never looked back. He walked from Easton to Wilmington, Delaware, then boarded a boat and took two trains. In later years, he would say that he finally stopped running after his arrival in Princeton, New Jersey only because that's where he ran out of money.

In freedom, he renamed himself James Collins Murphy. His wife, Phillis, a free black woman, and their son, Thomas, soon joined him in Princeton.

Murphy got a job as a janitor responsible for cleaning the dorm rooms and classrooms in Nassau Hall on the campus of Princeton College. Some of the tasks involved were none too pleasant—he had to keep the outhouses clean, for example, and some mean-spirited students saddled him with the nicknames "Jim Stink" and "James Odoriferous."

He had been living as a free man for four years when he was arrested on July 28, 1843 under the terms of that first Fugitive Slave Act of 1793. According to one report, Murphy resisted that arrest violently, even biting the finger of one man clear to the bone in the process.

The trial that followed was a high-profile affair, drawing so much public interest that it was held in the biggest hotel in downtown Princeton. Students from the South turned out as a makeshift private security force; they were worried that local blacks opposed to fugitive slave arrests might try to engineer a jailbreak.

In the end, Murphy was convicted. Before he could be returned to slavery in Maryland, however, a white woman from Princeton named Theodosia Ann Mary Prevost paid Severn Wallis $500 for Murphy's freedom. Princeton students took up a separate collection that netted $100 to help Murphy get back on his feet.

Murphy would repay his $500 debt to Prevost in relatively short order. He also would resume a career on the Princeton campus that would eventually cover six long decades. He moved on from that janitorial work in time and became a successful entrepreneur. He had a store that sold used clothing and furniture to students. He also had a food concession on campus. He seems to have had a knack for self-promotion, as he became known for the crazy costumes he would wear at sporting events while selling snacks out of a wooden cart.

His wife, Phillis, died in 1852. Murphy would marry a second time, then become a widower again, and marry a third time after that. His businesses hit on hard times in his later years, at which point students at Princeton once again took up a collection to help him out. Their fundraising appeal went like this:

> He has long been a feature of the campus and, now in his old age, we feel that he should be cared for by those whom he has known and who all remember him.

Murphy died in 1902. He is buried in historic Princeton Cemetery, sharing quarters with various U.S. presidents, vice presidents, generals, and other luminaries. The students at Princeton stepped up one last time on his behalf, taking up a collection to pay for a grave marker that identifies Murphy as "the students' friend."

TRAVEL RESOURCES

I have set the story of Moses Viney in Denton, Maryland, because that is roughly the location of that famous incident with the bloodhounds. (We will visit Viney's and Murphy's home turf of Talbot County soon enough in other chapters here centered on the life of Frederick Douglass.)

Information about things to do and places to go near Denton is available from **Caroline County Tourism**.
- Caroline Visitor Center, 5 Crouse Park Lane, Denton, Maryland

- TourCaroline.com;
  Facebook.com/CarolineTourism; 410.479.0655

The **Harriet Tubman Underground Railroad Byway** runs through both Dorchester and Caroline counties in Maryland and then on into Delaware.

- Maryland: HarrietTubmanByway.org;
  Facebook.com/HarrietTubmanByway;
  410.228.1000
- Delaware: TubmanBywayDelaware.org

18: 'I'm Sorry I'm Gwine to Lebe You' (Harriet's Escape, Part 2)

Greensboro, Maryland

BIG PICTURE
Strangers in a Strange Land

The first time I went looking for Red Bridges Road in Greensboro, Maryland, I got lost. I had checked Google Maps in advance, but my eye went straight to the line for a Red Bridges Road on the east side of the Choptank River, and I ended up wasting quite a bit of time roaming up and down Draper's Mill Road when I should have been on the west side of the river, along Greensboro Road.

It was a minor mishap, of course. This is the 21st century. I had a smart phone. I had plenty of gas. The nearby town of Greensboro is full of friendly folks who will happily help out a stranger.

I found my way soon enough to the right place, a little park hidden away at the end of a winding dirt road. Historians recommend a visit to Red Bridges because it's the kind of place where runaways might have crossed the Choptank River. The river isn't two miles wide here, like it is down in Cambridge. It's more of a creek, actually. You can stand on its banks here and imagine splashing across under the cover of darkness and ending up soaked only up to your thighs.

But my little mishap on the way there left me with another question: How would a slave in the 1840s know how to reach this spot? Some had conductors to guide them, of course. But oftentimes slaves ran away in complete ignorance of the simplest matters of geography: Where in the world is Pennsylvania? How far away is it? What towns lie along the way? What rivers need crossing?

This is, in fact, the state that Harriet Tubman seems to have been in on her first run for freedom. She and a couple of her brothers left without a conductor, or even much of a plan. They just started wandering north.

Standing with a cup of coffee on the banks of the Choptank at Red Bridges one winter morning, I tried to come up with a way to imagine their predicament. The best I could do was to imagine myself on the run from the powers that be in a foreign land. I picked the steppes of central Asia, actually, in the time of Genghis Khan and the Mongols.

I pictured in my mind's eye the way that vast landscape might look in the dark of night. Then I got to asking obvious things: What if heavy clouds obscured my view of a guiding star? What if the moon was too bright, making it hard to stay out of sight? What would I do if and when some wide, impassible river forced me to steer away from that guiding star? Was that the baying of bloodhounds I heard in the distance?

I had no map and no road signs and no cell phone. I imagined that the strangers in nearby towns were more likely to be dangerous foes than friendly souls. Would I have pressed on? Or would I have played it safe and turned back?

STORY
'I'm Sorry I'm Gwine to Lebe You'

As the summer of 1849 drew to a close, Harriet Tubman made the decision to run. Rumors were flying in the wake of her owner's recent death about the imminent sale of some of his slaves in order to pay off some of his debts. Tubman was not the sort of woman who was going to wait around in such circumstances. Those recurring dreams she had in which evil horsemen kept swooping down on her were only getting more intense.

Liberty or death: She would have one or the other.

In September, she convinced at least two and perhaps three of her brothers to join her in the flight to freedom. By the standards of most other slaves on the Eastern Shore, this was a reasonably worldly bunch. They knew their way around the shipyards in Madison. They had probably heard quite a bit through the Underground Railroad grapevine about the lay of the land and the turns in the river on the way north.

But they seem to have set off with no real preparation beyond wishful thinking. There is no indication that Tubman and her brothers ever made it all the way up to Red Bridges on this trip, but the point of setting this chapter at this particular spot is that it's the kind of place they *needed* to be able to find.

All they had, however, were those strange dreams and visions in Tubman's head, and perhaps that North Star up in the sky, if it wasn't too cloudy. According to the biographer Sarah Bradford, that first escape attempt ended this way:

> [T]hey had not gone far when the brothers, appalled by the dangers before and behind them, determined to go back, and in spite of her remonstrances, dragged her with them.

Knowing what we now know about how Harriet Tubman's story turned out, it's easy to jump to the conclusion that those brothers made a dumb decision. They were going back to a life in slavery and even, God forbid, the risk of getting sold off away from their family and loved ones.

But what if the brothers were right? What if their sister wasn't actually ready that first time out? What if she needed this sort of miserable failure in order to become the famed "Moses" of her people? If she and her brothers had gotten caught on that first blind flight, would Tubman ever have gotten the chance to cross into freedom?

The actions Tubman took after returning home from this failure imply that deep down she knew that her brothers had a point. She reached out quietly to the Underground Railroad network, telling a white neighbor about her situation, and about her plans to run.

No one knows for sure who that mysterious woman was, but the speculation centers on Hannah Leverton, a Quaker woman who lived with her husband, Jacob, outside of modern-day Preston and just a few miles away from the cabin of Tubman's parents on Poplar Neck.

In any case, the white woman gave Tubman a slip of paper with two names written on it. She also must have provided Tubman with directions to the first station on her journey. Tubman was so filled with gratitude toward this woman that she gave her a hand-stitched quilt as a gift.

It was only a few days after she and her brothers returned that Tubman decided to set out on her own, perhaps after hearing another rumor that she herself was headed to the auction block. She did not say goodbye to her mother. Instead, she offered to take on her mother's chore of milking cows so that Rit could quit working a little early that day and relax.

Tubman did seek out a friend named Mary, finding her in the kitchen of the home of slave owner Anthony C. Thompson, who owned much of the forestland on Poplar Neck. The room was too crowded with people for a private conversation, so Harriet coaxed Mary outside in hopes of finding a little privacy, but then Thompson himself rode up on a horse and Mary scurried back inside at the sight of him.

Tubman then stood outside and sang a song of farewell to Mary:

I'm sorry I'm gwine to lebe you,
Farewell, oh farewell;
But I'll meet you in the mornin',

Farewell, oh farewell.
I'll meet you in the mornin'.
I'm boun' for de promised land,
On the other side of Jordan,
Boun' for de promised land.

And she was off, alone this time. When she found her way to that first station and showed off the piece of paper with two names on it, the woman of the house told Tubman to grab a broom and start sweeping up. Tubman caught on quickly—this was a cover so that passersby or neighbors wouldn't get suspicious. Sometime after dark, that woman's husband told Harriet to climb into the bottom of his wagon. He then piled that wagon with enough supplies so that his human cargo would not be seen.

And that's it. We don't really know what happened after she got in that wagon. What other stations did she stop at? Which conductors helped her? Did she have any close calls? All we really know is that she was in Philadelphia soon enough.

Later, Tubman would describe her feelings at the end of this journey as a mix of elation and loneliness. What about her family back in Maryland?

To dis solemn resolution I came; I was free, and dey should be free also; I would make a home for dem in de North, and de Lord helping me, I would bring dem all dere. Oh, how I prayed den, lying all alone on the cold, damp ground: "Oh, dear Lord,"

I said, "I haint got any friend but you. Come to my help, Lord."

TESTIMONY
'Gloom and Melancholy Spread Through My Soul'

We have no way of knowing today exactly what happened on Tubman's first run to freedom, the one that ended with her brothers insisting that they give up and return home. But they may have endured the sort of anguish that James Pennington went through on the first night of his run to freedom. This is from his autobiography, *The Fugitive Blacksmith or, Events in the History of James W. C. Pennington, Pastor of a Presbyterian Church, New York, Formerly a Slave in the State of Maryland, United States.*

I now found myself under cover of night, a solitary wanderer from home and friends; my only guide was the North Star, by this I knew my general course northward, but at what point I should strike [Pennsylvania], or when and where I should find a friend, I knew not.

The night was fine for the season, and passed on with little interruption for want of strength, until, about three o'clock in the morning, I began to feel the chilling effects of the dew. At this moment, gloom and melancholy again spread through my whole soul. The prospect of utter destitution which threatened me was more than I could bear, and my heart began to melt.

What substance is there in a piece of dry Indian bread; what nourishment is there in it to warm the nerves of one already chilled to the heart? Will this afford a sufficient sustenance after the toil of the night?

But while these thoughts were agitating my mind, the day dawned upon me, in the midst of an open extent of country, where the only shelter I could find, without risking my travel by daylight, was a corn shock, but a few hundred yards from the road, and here I must pass my first day out. The day was an unhappy one; my hiding-place was extremely precarious. I had to sit in a squatting position the whole day, without the least chance to rest. But, besides this, my scanty pittance did not afford me that nourishment which my hard night's travel needed.

Night came again to my relief, and I sallied forth to pursue my journey. By this time, not a crumb of my crust remained, and I was hungry and began to feel the desperation of distress. As I traveled I felt my strength failing and my spirits wavered; my mind was in a deep and melancholy dream. It was cloudy; I could not see my star, and I had serious misgivings about my course.

POSTSCRIPT
The Point of a Gun

That first, ill-fated run for freedom with her brothers taught Tubman a few lessons that would come in handy down the road. First, planning is a plus, no matter how powerful the visions in your head. Second, flying solo can be foolish—the teamwork available along the Underground Railroad is the better option.

Third, runaways are bound to get cold feet along the way. Some of them are going to want to turn back, as her brothers had. But such second thoughts were fraught with risk for the entire enterprise of the Underground Railroad. A returning slave might be forced to reveal the identity of a conductor or the location of stations.

Once she became a conductor, Tubman adopted a zero-tolerance policy when it came to cold feet. She always carried a gun with her on her missions, and sometimes she needed to point that weapon at her own passengers, especially in those moments when they wanted to give up and go back home.

This is what Tubman would tell them: "You go on or die."

CONNECTIONS

- This is the second part of the story of Harriet Tubman's own flight to freedom. The first part is in Chapter 6.

TRAVEL RESOURCES

The crossing at Red Bridges is part of **Christian Park**, which is on Red Bridges Road just north of Greensboro along Greensboro Road. There are no amenities of note at this isolated little park, but it is a beautiful spot for a shady stroll along the banks of the Choptank in one of its skinniest stretches.

- 26041 Red Bridges Road, Greensboro, Maryland
- 410.479.8120

Information about things to do and places to go here in Caroline County is available from **Caroline County Tourism**.

- Caroline Visitor Center, 5 Crouse Park Lane, Denton, Maryland
- TourCaroline.com; Facebook.com/CarolineTourism; 410.479.0655

The **Harriet Tubman Underground Railroad Byway** runs through both Dorchester and Caroline counties in Maryland and then on into Delaware.

- Maryland: HarrietTubmanByway.org;
  Facebook.com/HarrietTubmanByway;
  410.228.1000
- Delaware: TubmanBywayDelaware.org

19: THE BIRTH OF FREEDOM

Tuckahoe Creek, Maryland

BIG PICTURE
Roots Run Deep

A good many abolitionists, black and white alike, supported a movement called "colonization" in the mid-1800s. The idea behind it was that once slaves became free, it would be best if they went back to Africa, the continent of their ancestors.

Colonization advocates even made some progress toward their goal. The movement helped create the modern-day nation of Liberia, which was founded by former American slaves.

Harriet Tubman was no fan of colonization. She viewed the idea in pretty much the same way third-generation members of many immigrant families today might react to the idea of moving back to the land of their ancestors—as crazy and out of the question. Tubman regarded herself more as an American than as an African immigrant.

In a speech to a meeting of abolitionists in Boston, she put it this way: "We're rooted here, and they can't pull us up."

Consider the case of another Eastern Shore native, Frederick Douglass. In the story that follows here, we will learn a bit about his childhood as a slave and how he came to spend a good deal of time at the Wye House plantation in Talbot County, Maryland. This was, and still is, the home of one of Maryland's most prominent white families, the Lloyds. The Lloyds date their history in the area to the late 1600s, when the first Edward

Lloyd arrived from Wales and began laying the foundation for a family fortune that would last for centuries.

By the time Fred Bailey (as Douglass was known in childhood) arrived at Wye House, the Lloyd fortune was in its fifth generation. But here is some food for thought: The Eastern Shore roots of the Bailey family ran just about as deep as those of the Lloyds. The historian Dickson J. Preston lays all this out in his book *Young Frederick Douglass: The Maryland Years*, tracing Fred Bailey's ancestry back through property, census, and tax records to a slave named Baly, whose earliest appearance in those records dates to 1746, at which point he was about 45 years old and the father of eight children.

Just like Edward Lloyd V, then, Fred Bailey was the fifth-generation descendant of an immigrant, albeit an enslaved one. That fact always comes into my mind when I run into the famous words Douglass spoke during the emotional visit he paid back to the area of his birth and childhood after Emancipation, in 1877.

I am an Eastern Shoreman, with all that name implies. Eastern Shore corn and Eastern Shore pork gave me my muscle. I love Maryland and the Eastern Shore.

STORY
The Birth of Freedom

Young Fred Bailey got his first taste of freedom when he was still too young to understand that a thing such as slavery existed. Later in life, he would describe the freewheeling nature of his first few years by comparing the life of a hypothetical slave child with that of a white counterpart:

[The slave child] seldom has to listen to lectures on propriety of behavior, or on anything else. He is never chided for handling his little knife and fork improperly or awkwardly, for he uses none. He is never reprimanded for soiling the table-cloth, for he takes his meals on the clay floor. He never has the misfortune, in his games or sports, of soiling or tearing his clothes, for he has almost none to soil or tear. He is never expected to act like a nice little gentleman, for he is only a rude little slave. ...

He literally runs wild; he has no pretty little verse to learn in the nursery, no nice little speeches to make for aunts, uncles, or cousins, to show how smart he is, and if he can only manage to keep out of the way of the heavy feet and fists of the older slave boys, he may trot on, in his joyous and roguish tricks, as happy as any little heathen under the palm trees of Africa. ...

In a word, he is, for the most part of the first

eight years of his life, a spirited, joyous, uproarious, and happy boy."

Little Fred passed these carefree if poverty-stricken years at Holme Hill, a farm in the countryside below the modern-day town of Queen Anne, Maryland. Historians place that site a little way southeast of the current intersection of Lewistown and Tappers Corner roads, but there is nothing really to see there today. The farmhouse of Fred's owner, Aaron Anthony, is gone. So is the cabin where Fred lived with his free grandfather, Isaac Bailey, and his enslaved grandmother, Betsy. The land is all privately owned in any case, so there is no opportunity to get out of a car and wander around.

For a taste of the freedom that young Fred Bailey enjoyed, I would recommend instead a visit to either Tuckahoe State Park or Adkins Arboretum, or both. In these adjacent parks a little bit north of Queen Anne, you'll still be able to take in the beauty of Tuckahoe Creek and wander the nearby woods and streams. It will be easy there to imagine the life of a little boy in the 1830s who spends pretty much all of his time wandering this paradise in search of fun and adventure. Here, too, it will be easy to picture a little cabin in the woods:

The old cabin, with its rail floor and rail bedsteads upstairs, and its clay floor downstairs and its dirt chimney and windowless sides ... and that most curious piece of workmanship, ... the ladder stairway, and the hole curiously dug in front of the fireplace, beneath which grandmammy placed the sweet potatoes in to keep them from the frosts, was MY HOME—the only home I ever had; and I loved it, and all connected with it.

Douglass did not recall spending much time in those years with his mother. She was always off working somewhere or another. He was too young at this point to be curious about the fact that his skin color was several shades lighter than hers, a fact that has long stoked speculation—still unconfirmed, as far as I can tell—that he was the son of his owner.

Slowly but surely Fred started to get a sense for the ways of the world, including the notion that the freedom he enjoyed in those early years would be a short-lived affair. He heard about his older siblings, for instance, but he had never met them—they were all off at some faraway place called Wye House. His master, Aaron Anthony, was there, too, working for the Lloyds as an overseer.

On a late summer day in 1824, Grandmammy Betsy packed up a few things and told Fred they were going on an adventure. At one point, Fred grew tired of walking, so 50-year-old Betsy hoisted him up on her shoulder, toting him like a "sack of wheat." You can trace the 12-mile route they may have taken to Wye House along country backroads, meandering along Tappers Corner and then Cordova, Longwoods, Sharp, and Todd's Corner roads before heading out towards

Bruffs Island.

Fred must have been astonished at what he saw here. Wye House was a place unlike most any other on the Eastern Shore, closer to a giant Deep South plantation than to the small family farms with a handful of slaves apiece that were so much more common in the area. Grandmammy Betsy likely led Fred right past the grand entry lane reserved for white folks of the upper crust, with its elaborate ornamental gate and half-mile-long canopy of decorative trees ending at the meticulously manicured "Long Green."

Instead, they would have taken the service road that lays a little way beyond that. It led through slave quarters that housed nearly 200 souls and had a whole city's worth of services—icehouse, blacksmith, carpenter, shoemaker, wheelwright, shipyard, windmill, milk house, and more.

Wye House, too, is privately owned and inaccessible to the public today, so there is no opportunity here for visitors to get out and stroll the grounds. Instead, you might consider wandering by car through the backroads of the surrounding Miles Neck area. Some of the farms and estates you'll pass have the look of old-time plantations. The small towns of Unionville and Copperville date their histories to earlier incarnations as slave quarter districts and free black communities in the time of Douglass and Tubman.

In Copperville, keep an eye out for a sign for Bailey Lane. The path it marks is just a little dirt alleyway, but the message it sends is about the deep roots that the family of Frederick Douglass has in the area—members of the Bailey clan are still living hereabouts today.

Upon arriving at Wye House after their long walk, Betsey introduced Fred to his siblings, a brother named Perry and sisters Sarah and Liza. The children all went off to play together, though Fred seems to have spent that time with his back to a wall, watching warily.

Then his grandmother was gone, headed back to Holme Hill without him. Fred howled in dismay at this realization. His brother Perry tried to console him with some fresh peaches and pears. Fred threw them to the ground and kept right on sobbing.

Things did not go well for Fred at Wye House. Interestingly, the bane of his existence was not some cruel slave master, but a fellow slave and family member, his Aunt Katy. The keeper of the kitchen, Katy either took a strong dislike to Fred or decided that he was in need of an extreme run of tough love. She refused to give him enough food—and sometimes any food at all.

She did nothing when other children pushed little Fred aside and stole his portion at mealtimes. Things got so bad that Fred endured desperate moments spent fending off dogs for scraps of leftovers and foraging in creeks for raw shellfish.

Unlike Aunt Katy, the Lloyd family seems to have taken a liking to Fred. Out of the 80 or so enslaved children on the plantation, he was chosen to be the special companion of young Daniel Lloyd. The two became fast friends for a time, exploring every nook and cranny of the farm together.

Some six months into Fred's time at Wye House, Harriet Bailey came to visit her son. Fred may not have spent much time with his mother up to that point, but he knew enough to trust her with an unvarnished account of his long mistreatment at the hands of Aunt Katy.

> I shall never forget the indescribable expression of her countenance. There was pity in her glance at me, and a fiery indignation at Aunt Katy at the same time.

Harriet consoled her son by giving him a piece of ginger cake. Then she turned to Aunt Katy and delivered a blistering rebuke, threatening to tell all to her master and condemning her for the "meanness" and "injustice" she had doled out to the child.

> That night I learned the fact that I was not only a child, but *somebody's* child. [I felt] prouder, on my mother's knee, than a king upon his throne.

When he woke up the next morning, his mother was gone. He would never see her again. The adult Frederick Douglass never knew his exact age, or the date of his birthday. After finding his way to freedom, he chose to celebrate the event each year on Valentine's Day, because he recalled how that piece of ginger cake his mother had given him was cut in the shape of a heart and that while holding him in her arms that night his mother had called him her "Valentine."

A few months after his mother's memorable visit, another keystone event took place in the life of young Fred Bailey. Word spread through the Bailey clan that two of their members, Jennie and Noah Bailey—they were Fred's aunt and uncle—had escaped and were trying to make a run for freedom in the North.

Historians who have looked into the case speculate that the couple knew, or at least suspected, that Aaron Anthony was about to put them up for sale. I find it impossible to imagine the turmoil that went into their decision to leave behind two small children, seven-year-old Mary and six-year-old Isaac.

Anthony posted a reward of $150 for Jennie and Noah, but they were never caught. Perhaps in reprisal for the couple's escape, Anthony soon sold those two young children to a slave trader from Alabama.

In time, word filtered back to the Bailey clan through an early version of the Underground Railroad grapevine that Jennie and Noah had indeed made it to the North and freedom. Looking back on this turn of events in later years, Douglass would see their escape as a first step on his own long journey to freedom. It was the first time he had ever heard that there were places where slaves could become free.

The success of Aunt Jennie and Uncle Noah in getting away from slavery was, I think, the first fact that made me seriously think of escape for

myself.... Young as I was, I was already, in spirit
and purpose, a fugitive from slavery.

TESTIMONY
'The Highest Joy and the Deepest Sadness'

As young Fred Bailey adjusted to life at Wye House, he
grew accustomed to the daily rituals of life on this
plantation-like farm. Everyone woke to a horn blown at
dawn, which was soon followed by a long parade of
slaves headed off to work, some at the great house,
others in the fields, and still others to the boatyard. He
was confused back then about the constant singing that
filled the fields and woods around him, but the import
of those sounds grew clearer in his mind as he grew
older and found his way to freedom. This is how he
recalled that singing by the slaves in *The Narrative of
the Life of Frederick Douglass*:

[The slaves] would make the dense old woods, for
miles around, reverberate with their wild songs,
revealing at once the highest joy and the deepest
sadness. They would compose and sing as they
went along, consulting neither time nor tune. The
thought that came up, came out—if not in the
word, in the sound—and as frequently in the one
as in the other. They would sometimes sing the
most pathetic sentiment in the most rapturous
tone, and the most rapturous sentiment in the
most pathetic tone. Into all of their songs they

would manage to weave something of the Great House Farm. Especially would they do this, when leaving home. They would then sing most exultingly the following words:
"I am going away to the Great House Farm!
O, yea! O, yea! O!"

This they would sing, as a chorus, words which to many would seem unmeaning jargon, but which, nevertheless, were full of meaning to themselves. I have sometimes thought that the mere hearing of those songs would do more to impress some minds with the horrible character of slavery, than the reading of whole volumes of philosophy on the subject could do.

I did not, when a slave, understand the deep meaning of those rude and apparently incoherent songs. I was myself within the circle; so that I neither saw nor heard as those without might see and hear. They told a tale of woe which was then altogether beyond my feeble comprehension; they were tones loud, long, and deep; they breathed the prayer and complaint of souls boiling over with the bitterest anguish. Every tone was a testimony against slavery, and a prayer to God for deliverance from chains. The hearing of those wild notes always depressed my spirit, and filled me with ineffable sadness. I have frequently found myself in tears while hearing them.

The mere recurrence to those songs, even now, afflicts me; and while I am writing these lines, an expression of feeling has already found its way down my cheek. To those songs I trace my first glimmering conception of the dehumanizing character of slavery. I can never get rid of that conception. Those songs still follow me, to deepen my hatred of slavery, and quicken my sympathies for my brethren in bonds. If any one wishes to be impressed with the soul-killing effects of slavery, let him go to Colonel Lloyd's plantation, and, on allowance-day, place himself in the deep pine woods, and there let him, in silence, analyze the sounds that shall pass through the chambers of his soul,—and if he is not thus impressed, it will only be because "there is no flesh in his obdurate heart."

I have often been utterly astonished, since I came to the north, to find persons who could speak of the singing, among slaves, as evidence of their contentment and happiness. It is impossible to conceive of a greater mistake. Slaves sing most when they are most unhappy. The songs of the slave represent the sorrows of his heart; and he is relieved by them, only as an aching heart is relieved by its tears. At least, such is my experience. I have often sung to drown my sorrow, but seldom to express my happiness. Crying for joy, and singing for joy, were alike uncommon to me while in the jaws of slavery. The singing of a man cast away upon a desolate island might be as appropriately considered as evidence of contentment and happiness, as the singing of a slave; the songs of the one and of the other are prompted by the same emotion.

CONNECTIONS

- The story of Fred Bailey's tumultuous journey through adolescence is the subject of Chapter 20.

TRAVEL RESOURCES

Here is information about visiting **Tuckahoe State Park**:
- 13070 Crouse Mill Road, Queen Anne, Maryland
- dnr2.maryland.gov/publiclands/Pages/eastern/Tuc kahoe.aspx; 410.820.1668

Here is information about visiting **Adkins Arboretum**:
- 12610 Eveland Road, Ridgely, Maryland
- AdkinsArboretum.org; 410.634.2847

While Douglass was born in Talbot County, the parks I suggest visiting here are just across the border in Caroline County. Information about things to do and places to go in Caroline County is available from **Caroline County Tourism**.
- Caroline Visitor Center, 5 Crouse Park Lane, Denton, Maryland

- TourCaroline.com;
  Facebook.com/CarolineTourism; 410.479.0655

Information about things to do and places to go in Talbot County is available from **Talbot County Tourism**. That office has a helpful driving tour brochure listing sites associated with the events in the life of Frederick Douglass.

- Talbot Visitor Center, 11 South Harrison Street, Easton, Maryland
- TourTalbot.org; 410.770.8000

The **Harriet Tubman Underground Railroad Byway** runs through both Dorchester and Caroline counties in Maryland and then on into Delaware.

- Maryland: HarrietTubmanByway.org;
  Facebook.com/HarrietTubmanByway;
  410.228.1000
- Delaware: TubmanBywayDelaware.org

20: THE FIGHT OF HIS LIFE

Wittman and St. Michaels, Maryland

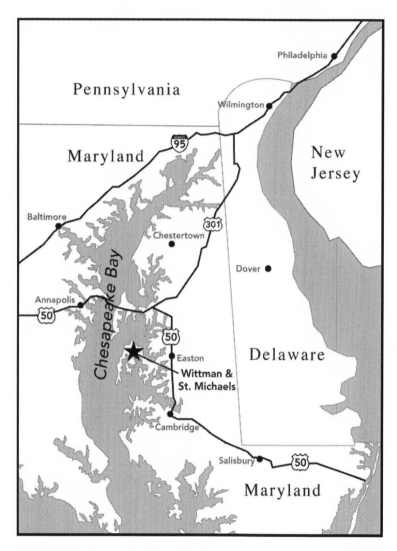

BIG PICTURE
The Auld Family Roller Coaster

Parenting experts tend to agree on the importance of consistency in child rearing. They say that an atmosphere where the rules are clear, and so are the consequences of breaking those rules, will help children through the growing pains they are bound to endure.

Young Fred Bailey had no such luck. Early on, the vagaries of slavery pulled him away from his own family. He never saw much of his mother before she died—he was still just a boy then. The time he spent with his siblings on the Lloyd plantation was brief, only a couple of years. Aside from a few early years in the care of his grandparents, Fred's upbringing was mostly in the hands of the white family that owned him.

That family went through its share of changes during Fred's younger years. His original owner, Aaron Anthony, shipped Fred off to Baltimore at the age of 8 to live with Hugh Auld, the brother of Anthony's son-in-law. After Anthony died the following year, Fred was inherited by Anthony's daughter, Lucretia, and her husband, Thomas Auld. They sent Fred back to Baltimore to live with Hugh for a while longer. By the time Fred returned to the Eastern Shore of Maryland, Lucretia had died and Thomas had a new wife, Rowena.

This rotating cast of caretakers gave Fred one mixed message after another. Arriving in Baltimore, 8-year-old Fred found himself wrapped up in the surprisingly warm embrace of Hugh's wife, Sophia, who had no prior experience caring for slaves and opted to welcome Fred into her home with a genuine, almost motherly affection. She even started teaching Fred the letters of the alphabet.

Those lessons came to an abrupt halt when the moodier, unpredictable "Master Hugh" learned about them and convinced his wife of the error of her ways with the slave boy. Later in life, after Fred had become the famous Frederick Douglass, he would recall how during his time in Baltimore, Sophia's "tender heart became stone, and [her] lamblike disposition gave way to one of tiger-like fierceness."

In his teens, Fred got caught in the middle of a spat between the two Auld brothers and was ordered to move to St. Michaels to live with his legal owner, Thomas, and his new wife, Rowena. There would be no stability waiting for Fred here, either. The emotional roller coaster ride he was on with the Auld family was about to get even more intense.

STORY
The Fight of His Life

Standing in downtown St. Michaels today, with its tourist-friendly bevy of upscale shops and interesting eateries, it's not easy to imagine the sort of place this town was when Frederick Douglass arrived in the early 1830s. Still known as Fred Bailey then, he was at this point a city boy through and through. He was horrified to find himself stuck in a rural backwater on Maryland's Eastern Shore.

Fred lived smack dab in the heart of downtown St. Michaels, near where Talbot Street, the main drag, intersects with Mill Street. There is a historic marker near that intersection, though no one knows where, precisely, the home of Thomas and Rowena Auld stood in this vicinity. The Aulds were a reasonably prominent family in the community. Thomas operated a store out of the front part of their house. He also served as the town's postmaster.

Whether through Fred's own boasting or by some other means, word soon got out among the blacks of St. Michaels that this newly arrived teen knew how to read and write. In Baltimore, Thomas Auld's sister-in-law, Sophia, had taught Fred a few basics about the alphabet. Fred then used his own smarts and creativity to parlay that smidgeon of knowledge into full-fledged literacy.

Here in St. Michaels, a man named Wilson asked Fred if he would teach some of the local blacks to read. Together, the two of them set about scavenging for some discarded old books and school texts that Fred could use in a makeshift classroom.

One Sunday shortly thereafter, some 20 students gathered in the home of a free black man, James Mitchell. They didn't try very hard to keep this session a secret. They were operating under the assumption that there was nothing illegal about blacks learning to read.

The next weekend, Fred and his students would find out otherwise.

There were quite a few reasons why many whites back then didn't want blacks to read. They feared literate blacks might be corrupted by all the abolitionist "propaganda" going around. They worried that runaway slaves might be able to forge free papers and travel passes.

Back up in Baltimore, when Hugh Auld had ordered his wife to stop teaching Fred the letters of the alphabet, he had said this:

A nigger should know nothing but to obey his master—to do as he is told to do. Learning would *spoil* the best nigger in the world. ... [T]here would be no keeping him. It would forever unfit him to be a slave. ... [And] it could do him ... a great deal of harm. It would make him discontented and unhappy.

Many white folks in St. Michaels, then, regarded the news of these reading classes as a threat. That next Sunday, a mob of whites armed with clubs and other weapons broke up the class. They claimed the authority of a 1723 law that prohibited "tumultuous meetings of slaves."

This turn of events put Thomas Auld in a difficult spot. A shopkeeper's livelihood depends on the goodwill of his customers, and many of those customers were now watching closely to see how Auld would handle this new slave who had showed up from the big city and commenced trying to teach "their" blacks to read.

Auld did not disappoint those neighbors. He hired Fred out for a one-year term to a farmer named Edward Covey, who had built a reputation for beating the rebelliousness out of even the most difficult slaves.

No doubt Fred was aware of Covey's reputation on New Year's Day, 1834, when he set off from the corner of Cherry and Talbot streets on the long seven-mile walk to his new home. You can trace Fred's steps today by following Route 33 out of town and into the countryside, passing first the turnoff for Neavitt and then the one for Claiborne, and then continuing right on through the little outpost of McDaniel until you come to New St. John's United Methodist Church on the left.

The Covey Farm is just across the road from here, on the Chesapeake Bay side. The land is private, so you can't go wandering about. There is nothing left of the Covey farmhouse and outbuildings in any case. In fact, those structures most likely stood on land that is now under water due to the one-two-three punch of erosion, subsidence, and rising sea levels.

Covey was 28 years old on that New Year's Day when Fred arrived. He stood 5 feet, 10 inches tall. His most notable features were a short neck, a "wolfish" face, and a voice that emerged from the side of his mouth in "a sort of light growl, like a dog, when an attempt is made to take a bone from him."

There were only three other slaves working on the small Covey farm, so there was no place for Fred to hide. To make matters worse, he had never worked as a field hand. Covey quickly set out to make a fool of Fred. He sent the newly arrived city boy out one day to chop some wood. The next, he gave him a wagon and a team of oxen so he could go fetch those bundles of chopped wood.

Fred went off that second day with no understanding of how hard it can be to manage a few thousand pounds of oxen. The beasts ran wild on him twice. After the first accident, Fred was able to put the pieces of his broken wagon back together. The second time, however, the oxen busted through a fence on Covey Farm, where the master soon discovered that a gate had been damaged because of Fred's lousy driving.

Covey whipped Fred for that.

Fred received quite a few more whippings in the days and weeks that followed. Covey was a devious, obsessive overseer, always popping up out of the blue at the most unexpected times in hopes of catching a slave slacking off or making a mistake.

He was under every tree, behind every stump, in every bush, and at every window on the plantation.

By midsummer, Fred's spirit was beaten. It might well have been the lowest point of his life.

I was broken in body, soul, and spirit. My natural elasticity was crushed, my intellect languished, the disposition to read departed, the cheerful spark that lingered about my eye died; the dark night of slavery closed in upon me; and behold a man transformed into a brute!

This bleak period found him gazing out toward the Chesapeake Bay on occasion, feeling great jealousy as the sails of passing vessels blew free in the distance. He was trying in those moments to hold onto the dream that he, too, might find a way to freedom, but the notion was slipping fast from his mind.

The Covey Farm nightmare came to a head during wheat-threshing season in August. Fred was hard at work in the fields one day when he collapsed, presumably suffering from heat stroke. Covey was having none of it. He kicked Fred's prone body and screamed at him to get up and get back to work.

When he finally came to, Fred made a run for it—not towards freedom, but back to St. Michaels where he might be able to plead for mercy from his owner, Thomas Auld. Auld listened to Fred's story, then ordered him to get out and walk those seven miles right back to Covey Farm.

Fred didn't return right away. He spent a desperate night in the woods, without food. An older black couple took him in. The man's name was Sandy, and he had managed to keep hold of his African folkways even after most of a lifetime in American slavery. Sandy dug up a root in the woods and promised Fred that it would protect him as long as he kept it in his right-hand pocket.

It was a Sunday when Fred showed up back at Covey Farm. For all his idle cruelty six days a week, Covey was a devout and careful observer of the Christian Sabbath. There would be no discipline on Fred's first day back.

Monday morning was a different story, however. Covey sent Fred into the horse stables and then set upon him in fury. He grabbed Fred by one leg and threw him to the ground. He tried to spin a noose around both of Fred's legs, but Fred scooted clear.

"Do you mean to resist, you scoundrel?"
"Yes, sir!"

Even much later in life, Fred could not really fathom "whence came the daring spirit."

Could the fight really have lasted two hours? That's how long the two men wrestled in Fred's memory many years later, in any case. Their battle spilled out of the stable and into the yard, where Covey demanded that another slave help him subdue the teenager. That slave declined to step in:

"My master hired me here to work, and not to help you whip Frederick."

It was Covey who broke off the battle and walked away, declaring victory and boasting to Fred about what would happen on their next go-round. But everyone who saw the fight knew that Covey had not won at all. He had not drawn even a drop of blood. He had not managed even one clear swing with his whip.

Fred, too, knew that Covey had not won the fight, that his claims of victory were nothing but idle boasts.

What happened next is hard to fathom: The slave breaker simply let the matter drop. For the last few months of Fred's term at the farm, Covey made no more efforts to discipline or whip him. He simply ignored Fred's existence altogether.

Had Covey really convinced himself that he'd won the fight and that was that? Or was it more complicated? Was he now afraid of Fred? Was he backing down? Or perhaps Thomas Auld had stepped in quietly here and told him to keep his hands off of Fred.

There is no telling the answers to these questions. What we can say is what was going on in Fred Bailey's mind.

I felt as I had never felt before. It was a glorious resurrection, from the tomb of slavery, to the heaven of freedom. My long-crushed spirit rose, cowardice departed, bold defiance took its place; and I now resolved that, however long I might remain a slave in form, the day had passed forever when I could be a slave in fact.

And:

This battle with Mr. Covey was the turning point in my life as a slave. I was NOTHING before: I WAS A MAN NOW.

Fred's time in the grip of the slave breaker came to a close on Christmas Day, 1834. At that point, the Auld family roller coaster took another surprising turn. The very same Thomas Auld who had so mercilessly sent Fred off to be broken on Covey Farm leased Fred's services for the following year to a farmer named William Freeland, whose reputation in dealing with slaves was one of fair play and gentle treatment.

Many years later, Frederick Douglass would recall Freeland as "the best master I ever had, until I became my own master." The time when Fred would be his own master was still quite a way off, however.

TESTIMONY
The White Sails of Freedom

While at his lowest point in the summer of 1834, Fred Bailey would look out to the western horizon from Covey Farm with a jumble of thoughts bouncing around in his mind.

Our house stood within a few rods of the Chesapeake Bay, whose broad bosom was ever white with sails from every quarter of the habitable globe.

Those beautiful vessels, robed in purest white, so delightful to the eye of freemen, were to me so many shrouded ghosts, to terrify and torment me with thoughts of my wretched condition. I have often, in the deep stillness of a summer's Sabbath, stood all alone upon the lofty banks of that noble bay, and traced, with saddened heart and tearful eye, the countless number of sails moving off to the mighty ocean.

The sight of these always affected me powerfully. My thoughts would compel utterance; and there, with no audience but the Almighty, I would pour out my soul's complaint, in my rude way, with an apostrophe to the moving multitude of ships:

"You are loosed from your moorings, and are free; I am fast in my chains, and am a slave! You move merrily before the gentle gale, and I sadly before the bloody whip! You are freedom's swift-winged angels, that fly round the world; I am confined in bands of iron! O that I were free! O, that I were on one of your gallant decks, and under your protecting wing! Alas! Betwixt me and you, the turbid waters roll.

"Go on, go on. O that I could also go! Could I but swim! If I could fly! O, why was I born a man, of whom to make a brute! The glad ship is gone; she hides in the dim distance. I am left in the hottest hell of unending slavery. O God, save me! God, deliver me! Let me be free! Is there any God?

Why am I a slave? I will run away. I will not stand it. Get caught, or get clear, I'll try it. I had as well die with ague as the fever. I have only one life to lose. I had as well be killed running as die standing.

"Only think of it; one hundred miles straight north, and I am free! Try it? Yes! God helping me, I will. It cannot be that I shall live and die a slave. I will take to the water. This very bay shall yet bear me into freedom. ...Meanwhile, I will try to bear up under the yoke. I am not the only slave in the world. Why should I fret? I can bear as much as any of them. [And] it may be that my misery in slavery will only increase my happiness when I get free. There is a better day coming."

CONNECTIONS

- Within a few months of the fight described here, Fred Bailey would be plotting his first run for freedom. That story is in Chapter 21.

TRAVEL RESOURCES

St. John's United Methodist Church, where the parking lot offers a view toward the old Covey Farm and the Chesapeake Bay, is at 9123 Tilghman Island Road in Wittman, Maryland—that's about six miles beyond St. Michaels on Route 33. The land that you will be looking out over between there and the water is private property, inaccessible to the public. Also, the Covey Farm site is actually underwater at this point, a victim of the one-two-three punch of erosion, land subsidence, and sea-level rise.

Another option where you can take in the sort of view that young Fred Bailey had when looking out at those white sails of freedom is the **Claiborne Landing boat launch**. Claiborne Road is between the Covey Farm site and the town of St. Michaels. Take it north from Route 33 until you get into town, then stay left at Claiborne Landing Road, following it to the water.

The Covey Farm site and Claiborne Landing are both near the town of St. Michaels, which is full of interesting shops and restaurants. It is also home to the excellent Chesapeake Bay Maritime Museum. The **St. Michaels Business Association** is a good place to find information about things to do and places to go while there.

- stmichaelsmd.org; 410.745.0412

As of this writing in 2017, **the St. Michaels Museum** at St. Mary's Square has a number exhibit panels and other materials related to Frederick Douglass. They also offer occasional guided walking tours on the theme of Douglass's time in St. Michaels.

- 201 East Chestnut Street, St. Michaels, Maryland
- StMichaelsMuseum.org; 410.745.9561

More information about things to do and places to go in St. Michaels and nearby towns is available from **Talbot County Tourism**. That office also has a helpful driving tour brochure listing sites associated with events in the life of Frederick Douglass.

- Talbot Visitor Center, 11 South Harrison Street, Easton, Maryland
- TourTalbot.org; 410.770.8000

21: A Long and Desperate Walk in Chains

St. Michaels and Easton, Maryland

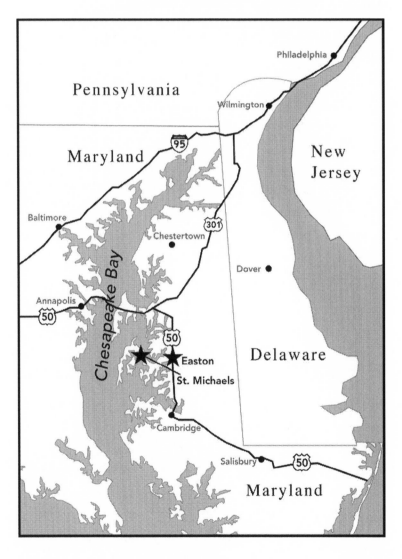

BIG PICTURE
Dreaming at 17

As we put on a few years in life, there are things from our younger days that tend to get a little fuzzy in our memories. Can we really still relate to what it's like to be 17 years old, smart as a whip and handsome as all get out? Can we still relate to what's going on inside such a young man, poised on the brink of adulthood with a heart full of passion and a head full of big dreams?

That's pretty much where Fred Bailey was in life when he made his first run for freedom. He knew deep down that he was going to be the hero of this adventure, that he would be the one to lead his best pals to freedom. As we shall see, things didn't quite go according to plan.

STORY
A Long and Desperate Walk in Chains

Along Route 33 just beyond St. Michaels, Maryland, there is an intersection with little Broad Creek Road. Fred Bailey was 17 when he arrived at this crossroads, bound for a farm just to the south, on the shores of a creek with the same name as the street.

Fred had developed a bit of a reputation for himself by this point. After arriving in St. Michaels from the big city, he had promptly set about trying to teach some local blacks to read. That didn't go over very well with hardliners in the white community—they shut his school down after one lesson.

Fred was then sent off to a year of service with an infamous slave breaker, Edward Covey. That ordeal came to a rousing conclusion in a no-holds-barred fistfight pitting the young slave against his would-be breaker. The fight ended in something of a draw, but that was enough for Fred to emerge as the clear winner in the eyes of his fellow slaves.

Now his owner, Thomas Auld, was hiring him out to this new farm. Here, his master would be William Freeland, a man with a reputation for treating slaves with a measure of honesty and fairness. The other slaves at Freeland Farm had heard through the grapevine about Fred's recent fistfight. From the get-go, they looked to him as a leader. Fred started up another secret school here, but this time he did a much better job of hiding it. Classes were in the woods one day, behind a barn the next, and so on.

That first Christmas at Freeland, Fred enjoyed his first taste of alcohol and may even have over-imbibed a bit. Later in life, he would develop a reputation as a strict teetotaler. As a teenager, however, he thoroughly enjoyed the homemade applejack brandy that his new master passed out to slaves during the holiday.

The time off that slaves enjoyed at Christmas could stretch on for a few days. According to bits of oral history, at least some masters on the Eastern Shore let the holiday last for as long as a special "Yule log" would burn in the master's fireplace. Legend has it that slaves looking to extend their time off would soak special logs in watery marshlands for months in advance, retrieving them for delivery on Christmas Eve.

On New Year's Day, Fred made a resolution: He would escape slavery before the end of the coming year, 1836.

Five co-conspirators signed on with him. They held secret meetings every Sunday night. The plan they hatched involved stealing a log canoe from a neighboring farm and sailing it down Broad Creek, out the Choptank River, and into the Chesapeake Bay. From there, they would head north until it seemed like time to ditch the boat and make an overland dash for the Pennsylvania border.

This all sounds perfectly plausible to our 21st century minds familiar with modern-day maps. But Fred Bailey and his co-conspirators had only the vaguest notion of where this thing called Pennsylvania might be. Their minds soon filled with all manner of frightening images from the unknown territory ahead.

Upon either side, we saw grim death assuming a variety of horrid shapes. Now, it was starvation, causing us, in a strange and friendless land, to eat our own flesh. Now, we were contending with the waves, ... and were drowned. Now, we were hunted by dogs, and overtaken and torn to pieces by their merciless fangs. We were stung by scorpions—chased by wild beasts—sleeping in the woods—suffering hunger, cold, heat, and nakedness—we supposed ourselves to be overtaken by hired kidnappers, who, in the name of the law, and for their ... accursed reward, would, perchance, fire upon us—kill some, wound others, and capture all.

The team lost a member along the way. An older slave named Sandy dropped out, citing his fear of getting captured.

As the others pressed on, they grew positively giddy with the approach of the appointed day, Easter Sunday. The mere sight of each other while going about their work on Freeland Farm would cause the co-conspirators to break into song:

"O Canaan, sweet Canaan! I am bound for the land of Canaan!"

The day before Easter, all was ready. Packs of food and clothes were hidden away. Fred had forged handwritten passes. That log canoe had been liberated and then beached in an out-of-the-way location.

Then, out of the blue, everything went south. Fred was called back out of the fields. Approaching the house at Freeland Farm, he saw half a dozen white men on horseback. One was the owner of that log canoe, William Hambleton. Among the others were armed constables.

They had been betrayed by that man who backed out, Sandy. This development was unfathomable to Fred, who regarded Sandy as an old and trusted friend. Fred was soon bound with rope and brought into the kitchen. One of his co-conspirators, Henry Harris, was brought in as well. When the constables told Henry to extend his hands so they could tie him up, he exploded in frustration.

"No, I won't!" Henry screamed.

Two of the constables pulled guns.

"You can't kill me but once," Henry said. "Shoot! Shoot and be damned! I won't be tied."

Henry pushed away at least one of the guns, sending it flying out of the hands of a constable and skittering across the room. He was soon subdued, and beaten.

Somewhere in the midst of this melee, Fred managed to take his forged pass and throw it into a fireplace without anyone noticing.

When things had settled down, a black woman named Betsey Freeland appeared on the scene. She was bringing biscuits to her two captured sons, Henry and John. The mother pinned their predicament square on Fred's influence, and she let him have it:

> You devil! You yellow devil! It was you that put it into the heads of Henry and John to run away. But for you, you long legged yellow devil, Henry and John would never have thought of running away.

On her way outside, Betsey unleashed a "scream of mingled wrath and terror."

The accusation must have unnerved Fred, but he managed to keep his wits about him. Tied behind a pair of horses, the conspirators were marched off of the farm and on toward St. Michaels. On the way, Fred whispered to his compatriots that they should "own nothing" and claim innocence.

The biscuits Betsey had delivered came in handy. The conspirators passed those treats around, with each one using it as an opportunity to put his own forged pass in his mouth and swallow it. Now, there was no physical evidence whatsoever tying them to an escape plot.

In St. Michaels, the suspects were led into a makeshift interrogation room, where Fred took the lead in pleading their case:

[N]othing has been done! We have not run away. We were quietly at our work. Where is the evidence against us?

Next came a long march to Easton, 12 miles away. The next time you're traveling along Route 33 between those two towns, try to put the scene that unfolded that day in your mind's eye. Word of the aborted escape attempt had spread through the countryside. White people in communities along the way—Spencer's Cove, Royal Oak, Miles Ferry, more—came out on the roadside to aim jeers and insults at this "yellow devil" they'd heard about, and at his companions.

That long walk ended at the jail in downtown Easton at the corner of West and Federal streets. (The jail there today was built in 1878, but the previous one was in the same spot.) Sitting inside, Fred Bailey mulled over the state of those big dreams he had at age 17. That vision he had of himself as the heroic leader of a dramatic odyssey to freedom in the "land of Canaan" was gone now. Instead, he expected that he would end up at a cotton plantation in Georgia or some other god-forsaken place in the Deep South. The door to his cell opened, and

> [in came] a swarm of imps in human shape—the slave-traders, deputy slave-traders, and agents of slave-traders—that gather in every country town of the state, waiting for chances to buy human flesh, as buzzards to eat carrion.

They poked and prodded Fred all over, rubbing his arms, checking his legs, and inspecting his stomach muscles.

Fred and his co-conspirators sat in the jail for three long days. On Tuesday, William Freeland showed up with his neighbor, William Hambleton. They took the four other conspirators away, but left Fred alone, still behind bars. Oddly, it seems that none of the other four were severely punished—they were just sent back to work as if nothing had happened.

Fred's owner, Thomas Auld, left him alone in that jail for four more days. When he did show up to escort Fred away, he announced that he had arranged to sell Fred to a friend in Alabama. Fred didn't believe it. He knew Auld's affairs pretty well after all these years. He didn't recall ever hearing about any friends in Alabama.

Auld did not take Fred back to Freeland Farm. After a few days in his St. Michaels home, the owner took his young slave to a nearby steamboat wharf and loaded him on a boat bound for Baltimore. He told Fred he was sending him back into the care of his brother, Hugh, and Hugh's wife, Sophia. Fred had mostly loved the time he spent in his younger years at Hugh's home in the Fells Point neighborhood. This seemed to him more like a reward than a punishment.

Thomas Auld seems to have gone through quite a bit of turmoil trying to decide what to do in the wake of Fred's participation in the conspiracy. He was under a lot of pressure from his neighbors to sell Fred away; one neighbor had even threatened to shoot Fred dead if he ever saw him again.

Here is a tidbit Fred heard later from a cousin of his:

Master Thomas was very unhappy [that whole week]; and that the night before his going up to release me [from the jail], he had walked the floor nearly all night, evincing great distress.

The grapevine also carried word to Fred that some of those slave traders had indeed made offers to buy him.

Auld had rejected those offers. Now he was sending Fred back to Baltimore. Is it possible that Thomas didn't realize that Fred was sure to make another run for freedom, and soon? I'd doubt it. My guess is that Auld just decided to leave the matter be, for reasons that will always remain shrouded in mystery.

TESTIMONY
On the Block

While a young slave in North Carolina, W.L. Bost watched from a distance as slaves went up on the auction block. This is the sort of future Fred Bailey expected in his own life while being poked and prodded by those slave traders who came to see him in the Easton jailhouse.

Bost was interviewed by a writer working on a collection of slave narratives for the Federal Writers' Project in the 1930s. His narrative appears in *When I Was a Slave: Memoirs from the Slave Narrative Collection*.

The speculators stayed in the hotel and put the niggers in the quarters just like droves of hogs. All through the night I could hear them mournin' and prayin'. I didn't know the Lord would let people live who were so cruel.

I remember when they put 'em on the block to sell 'em. The ones 'tween eighteen and thirty always bring the most money. The auctioneer he stand off at a distance and cry 'em off as they stand on the block.

I can hear his voice as long as I live. If the one they going to sell was a young Negro man this is what he says: "Now gentlemen and fellow citizens here is a big black buck Negro. He's stout as a mule. Good for any kind o' work and he never gives any trouble. How much am I offered for him?"

And then the sale would commence and the nigger would be sold to the highest bidder. If they put up a young nigger woman, the auctioneer cry out: "Here's a young nigger wench, how much am I offered for her?" The poor thing stand on the block a shiverin' and a shakin' nearly froze to death. The poor mothers beg the speculators to sell 'em with their husbands, but the speculator only take what he want. So maybe the poor thing never see her husband again.

CONNECTIONS

- A more detailed account of the events leading up to Fred's fistfight with the slave breaker that is mentioned here is in Chapter 20.
- Fred Bailey did indeed make another run for it from Baltimore. The story of how he finally found his way to freedom is in Chapter 28.
- Many years after the Civil War, Frederick Douglass returned to St. Michaels and had a cordial meeting

of reconciliation with his former owner, Thomas Auld. That story is in Chapter 22.

TRAVEL RESOURCES

There is nothing in the way of public spaces or amenities in the immediate vicinity of the old Freeland Farm site. It was in the vicinity of the intersection of Broad Creek Road and Route 33. If you want to get a good look at the mouth of **Broad Creek**, take the pretty ride down nearby Route 579, Bozman Neavitt Road, until it ends at a boat launch.

Information about things to do and places to go in St. Michaels, Easton, and nearby towns is available from **Talbot County Tourism**. That office also has a helpful driving tour brochure listing sites associated with events in the life of Frederick Douglass.

- Talbot Visitor Center, 11 South Harrison Street, Easton, Maryland
- TourTalbot.org; 410.770.8000

22: FREDERICK DOUGLASS COMES BACK HOME

St. Michaels and Easton, Maryland

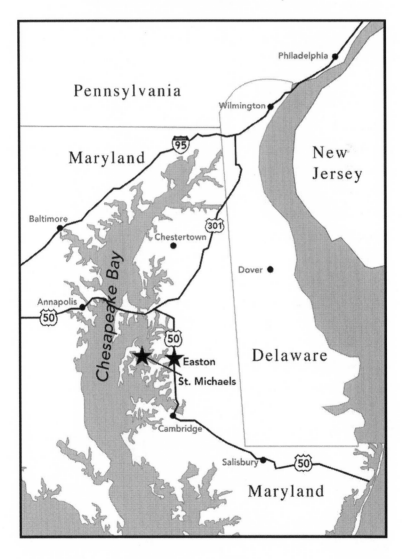

BIG PICTURE
The Aging Rock Star

There is an arc to the life story of Frederick Douglass that will be familiar to fans of modern-day pop music. How many rock stars come out of the gate raging furiously against the soulless confines of small-town or suburban life, only to end up years later turning out affectionate and nostalgic tunes about days gone by?

While he would never grow nostalgic for the days of slavery, Douglass nevertheless followed a 19th century version of this arc. As the years piled up after the Civil War, the fury of his younger self gave way to a tendency toward nuance and thoughtfulness in his writing and speeches. He was often extending olive branches to former foes. A lot of people back then admired the way he turned himself into this type of elder statesman. More than a few hard-core activists, however, complained that he had gone soft in his old age.

Douglass spent the bulk of his life in freedom and living up north. Those years are as full of interesting twists and turns as his time in Maryland. Little Fred Bailey, born in a cabin on Tuckahoe Creek, would become the most famous and honored black man of his time. The media would follow his every step. He would serve in the then-prominent post of U.S. marshal in Washington, D.C. He would be appointed U.S. ambassador to Haiti. Whispers about a possible run for the U.S. Senate would follow him to his deathbed.

Needless to say, then, the plans he made in 1877 to return to St. Michaels and pay a call on his former master, Thomas Auld, elicited great interest across a country that was still early on in its journey to try and come to terms with the legacy of slavery in the aftermath of the Civil War.

STORY
Frederick Douglass Comes Back Home

That 1877 trip was not the first time Douglass returned to Maryland. Thirteen years before, he had visited Baltimore just 16 days after the adoption of a new state constitution that outlawed slavery. He gave half a dozen speeches in various parts of the city on that trip. In his mid-fifties by this point, Douglass talked at every turn about how he wanted "not to condemn the past but to comment and rejoice over the present."

For me, the most interesting detail of the trip is the fact that Douglass made a quiet inquiry about perhaps paying a visit to Sophia Auld, the sister-in-law of his owner. Sophia had been his de facto mistress during the years he lived in Baltimore.

These two had a complex relationship. When Fred was a boy, Sophia had showered him with motherly affection and kindness, even going so far as to begin teaching him the letters of the alphabet, until her husband found out and ordered her to stop. In his later writings, Douglass often commends Sophia for her kindnesses, but he also portrays her as a woman who changed over time, becoming harder and even cruel toward him. She is the poster child in his books for the idea that the institution of slavery could corrupt even the most generous of white hearts.

Sophia flat-out refused to see Douglass on that 1864 visit. The question is why: Was she just being cruel, a bit of a sore loser, or did she feel justified in turning him away?

In 1848, back when he was still a young rising star in abolitionist circles, Douglass had penned an essay for his own newspaper, *The North Star*, titled "Letter to My Old Master." In it he promised:

I intend to make use of you as a weapon with which to assail the system of slavery ... as a means of bringing this guilty nation, with yourself, to repentance.

There is no question but that Douglass was on the noble and just side of the fight against slavery, but there are questions about the way he went about wielding the members of the Auld family as public-relations weapons in that fight.

Clearly, there were times when he exaggerated things about the Aulds. Some historians suspect that his portrayal of the hardening of Sophia's heart over the years may be one such case. There is no doubt about another case, a false accusation that Thomas Auld had abandoned Douglass's beloved grandmother in her old age. In fact, Auld had treated her quite generously by the standards of the time.

Douglass penned three different autobiographies in his life. If you compare them in sequence, you can get a sense for how he began to regret some of his more outrageous charges and rhetoric as time went on. The accusations he levels against the Aulds in his first book get toned down a notch in the second and then softened even more in the third.

Douglass turned down an invitation to return to the Eastern Shore shortly after the Civil War and participate in the town of Easton's Fourth of July festivities in 1867. He cited a prior engagement and sent along a very funny note of regret that included a reference to how the last time he had visited Easton he had been obliged to stay for while in a house decorated with "heavy locks, thick walls, iron gratings, and unwholesome atmosphere."

It was a decade later, in 1877, that Douglass heard through the grapevine that his old master, Thomas Auld, was in ill health and might not live much longer. That June 17, a Sunday, Douglass was aboard the steamship *Matilda* when it arrived at Navy Point in St. Michaels.

Today, the spot where that vessel docked is a part of the campus of the first-rate Chesapeake Bay Maritime Museum. They have an entire building devoted to the history of steamboats like *Matilda*, along with lots of other exhibits and materials about the various shipbuilding and maritime traditions that shaped the life of Frederick Douglass and so many other admirable men and women through the centuries.

On the afternoon of his arrival, Douglass delivered a talk to a mixed audience of blacks and whites, but such speechifying was a secondary goal on this trip, as Douglass made clear while speaking with a reporter from the *Baltimore Sun.*

I come, first of all, to see my old master, from whom I have been separated for forty-one years, to shake his hand, to look into his kind old face.

Soon enough then, Douglass made his way to the home of William and Louisa Bruff. Today, that building is known as the "Dodson House," and it's located just up Cherry Street from the maritime museum. It's been functioning as a bed and breakfast since the 1990s.

Louisa was a daughter from Thomas Auld's second marriage. She and William, a judge by trade, were the ones taking care of her bedridden father. The Bruffs welcomed Douglass through the front door, which counted in those days as a rather magnanimous gesture on their part toward a black man, and then led him into the bedroom where his former master lay.

The two exchanged the simplest of greetings:

"Captain Auld!"
"Marshal Douglass!"

The next exchange between the two men would end up being the subject of a silly media controversy. Douglass broke the formality of the moment by telling Auld to go ahead and address him as "Fred," as he had been known back in the day. Douglass took heat for this from some of his old abolitionist buddies—they thought he was being overly subservient to a slave owner he had once excoriated.

To make matters worse, a report in the *Baltimore Sun* claimed that Douglass at some point in this visit "grasped the palsied hand of Captain Auld [and] begged for his forgiveness." A Southern newspaper had great fun with this, publishing a widely circulated cartoon showing the great Frederick Douglass down on his knees before his former master.

Douglass would later dismiss all this noise as "the work of heartless triflers," and he would explain that he was apologizing to Auld not in some general way, but for the very specific offense of getting things wrong in that false accusation about the abandonment of his grandmother. Back in the moment, Douglass kept his focus squarely on the ailing man before him.

The sight of him, the changes which time had wrought in him, his tremulous hands constantly in motion, and all the circumstances of his condition affected me deeply, and for a time choked my voice and made me speechless. We both, however, got the better of our feelings, and conversed freely about the past.

At one point, Douglass asked Auld how he felt when receiving the news those many years ago that young Fred Bailey had run away for good. This led to a genuine, and seemingly heartfelt moment of reconciliation on both sides.

> "Frederick, I always knew you were too smart to be a slave, and had I been in your place, I should have done as you did."
>
> "Captain Auld, I am glad to hear you say this. I did not run away from *you* but from *slavery*; it was not that I loved Caesar less, but Rome more."

After that visit, Douglass gave another speech in St. Michaels, sounding themes quite akin to modern-day self-help gurus and urging his fellow blacks to work hard and save money. The *New York Times* was not impressed:

> It would appear that Mr. Fred. Douglass's role as a leader of his race is about played out.

The following year, Douglass arrived in Easton aboard the steamboat *Highland Light* to give a lecture sponsored by the local Republican party. He stayed in the fancy Brick Hotel, which occupied a building that had once housed Lowe's Tavern, a watering hole known to be quite popular with slave traders.

Douglass gave his speech at the courthouse before an audience that was mixed, but segregated, with blacks and whites seated in separate sections of the room. Once again, the man who rose to fame through the force of his fiery abolitionist rhetoric went out of his way to make a generous gesture of reconciliation, singling out one member of the audience, the former Sheriff Joseph Graham, for giving him "kindly treatment" during the days he spent behind bars at the nearby Easton Jail in his younger years.

The speech Douglass gave is a variation on one of his standard lectures, "Self-Made Men." It included tributes to famous examples of the title type, including Abraham Lincoln, Horace Greeley, and Benjamin Banneker. He once again urged blacks to embrace the virtues of hard work and financial responsibility. He told whites that it was time to accept the fact that blacks would be going to school and church now—and that black men would be going into the voting booth.

Just like on his earlier visit to St. Michaels, however, the speechifying that Douglass did while in Easton is less interesting than what he did in his free time. In Easton, he hired a wagon to take him on the 12-mile journey up to the stretch of Tuckahoe Creek where he had been born sixty-some years before.

His grandmother's cabin was long gone. There weren't even any traces left of the farmhouse of his initial owner, Aaron Anthony. Douglass had a devil of a time finding the location of his old cabin home. He had to go tromping into the brush at one point in search of an old cedar tree that would help him be 100 percent sure he was in the right spot.

When he found that spot at last, he commenced scooping up several handfuls of Tuckahoe dirt, which he would bring back to his home in Washington, D.C., as a remembrance of the place where his long journey through life had begun.

Douglass would make a couple more visits to the Eastern Shore before his death in 1895. In 1881, he visited Wye House, the plantation of Lloyds where he had toiled for several years as a child. Then, in 1893, he made a quiet last visit to Easton and St. Michaels amid rumors that he was thinking about buying a home in the area. It was a rumor that Douglass shot down.

I came to drink water from the old-fashioned well that I drank from many years ago, to see the few of the old friends that are left of the many I once had, to stand on the old soil once more before I am called away by the great Master, and to thank Him for his many blessings to me during my checkered life.... [T]hat's all I came for.

CONNECTIONS

- The story of the time young Fred Bailey spent along Tuckahoe Creek in childhood is in Chapter 19.
- The story of Douglass's own escape to freedom is in Chapter 28.
- The complexities of Douglass's relationship with the Auld family are touched on in Chapter 20 and Chapter 21.

TRAVEL RESOURCES

The first-rate **Chesapeake Bay Maritime Museum** occupies the site of the old steamboat landing where Douglass disembarked in St. Michaels.

- 213 North Talbot Street, St. Michaels, Maryland
- cbmm.org; 410.745.2916

In Easton, there is a statue on the lawn of the **Talbot County Courthouse** downtown that depicts Douglass in the act of giving his "Self-Made Men" speech in that same building in 1878.

- 11 North Washington Street, Easton, Maryland

Information about things to do and places to go in St. Michaels is available from the **St. Michaels Business Association**.

- stmichaelsmd.org; 410.745.0412

Information about attractions and businesses in Easton and St. Michaels is available through **Talbot County Tourism**.

- Talbot Visitor Center, 11 South Harrison Street, Easton, Maryland
- TourTalbot.org; 410.770.8000

23: SIDE TRIP: THE OXFORD WATERFRONT

Oxford, Maryland

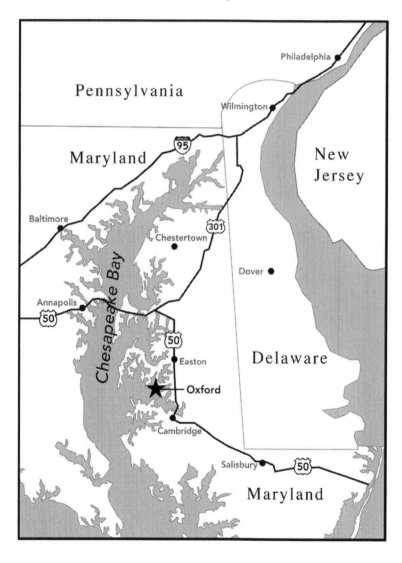

The little town of Oxford on the Tred Avon River is chock full of history. There was a time back in the early 1700s when the colonial powers that be thought sure that Oxford was going to grow up to be the biggest trading center on the Eastern Shore of Maryland.

For a while there, it looked like those prognostications would turn out to be true. By the mid-1700s, the town's port was hosting as many as seven or eight large trading ships at a time, with cargo coming in from pretty much every corner of the world.

Human cargo was part of the deal. On occasion, that cargo came into Oxford aboard large slave ships filled with enslaved West Africans from what we now know as the nation of Senegal. In 1770, the British ship *Lancaster* dropped off 124 slaves here after picking up 140 people in Senegal. The next year, *Success Packet* dropped off 104 slaves after picking up 134. The year after that, *Success Packet* returned, delivering 86 slaves after picking up 110.

The 70 souls who boarded those three ships in Senegal but didn't make it to Oxford represent nearly 20 percent of the total. It's possible that some of those souls were sold at ports along the way. It's more likely that most of them died during the horrific journey.

More often, it was simple merchant ships that brought new slaves into town, not the big slavers of Middle Passage infamy. These vessels would pick up a handful of slaves at a time while loading a variety of other goods from ports in the West Indies. For a while in this early period, there was apparently a good trade in white indentured servants and convicts from Ireland and Scotland, too.

Oxford had a reputation early on as a reasonably cultured place, at least by the standards of the isolated Eastern Shore. But there are hints in the historical record of a darker side. In *Talbot County: A History*, Dickson J. Preston paraphrases and then quotes the words of ship captain Jeremiah Banning:

> It was not uncommon in those days for people "of the first class" to get together and boast of new and ingenious ways of whipping Negroes. "And I am sorry to say," [Banning said], "that the ladies would too often mingle in the like conversation, and seem to enjoy it."

Today, the port of Oxford is mainly a center for recreational boating. The town's modern-day economy is built on tourism first and foremost, with a steady stream of visitors drawn by one of the prettiest waterfronts on the Delmarva Peninsula, as well as an abundance of stately old buildings and trees. It's a stroller's paradise.

Oxford is 12 miles from Easton by car, but in the warmer months it's much more fun to find your way there from the Tred Avon River waterfront at Bellevue via a ferry crossing that ranks among the oldest such services in the country. Right near where that ferry lands in Oxford, there is a historic marker that tells how the story of slavery in Oxford came full circle in the end.

The Emancipation Proclamation of January 1, 1863 freed slaves throughout the Confederate states but did not change the status of the slaves in Union states like Maryland where slavery was still legal. However, it did authorize the Union Army to recruit and enlist slaves, who then received promises of a bit of bonus money, plus freedom upon discharge for themselves and their families.

Union General William Birney set up shop here in Oxford soon thereafter, recruiting slaves for the various colored regiments then being put together. One such mission unfolded on September 18, 1863 when the steamboat *Champion* departed Oxford loaded with new recruits. A Quaker man named James Dixon was an observer that day:

> The [slave] owners and others stood silent and thoughtful upon the wharf and beach, and as the steamer moved off, the colored people on board, waving their hats in good bye, broke out into one of their jubilant hymns, such as they were accustomed to sing in their religious meetings, for having no patriotic songs those hymns were converted into songs of deliverance from slavery.

A number of local slaves ended up serving in the 19th regiment of the U.S. Colored Troops. That unit participated in Civil War battles and skirmishes in Florida, South Carolina, and Virginia before ending up at Appomattox Court House for the surrender of Confederate General Robert E. Lee.

CONNECTIONS

- In the Testimony section of Chapter 1, you can read a firsthand account of what it was like to be aboard a slave ship on the Middle Passage journey from West Africa in the mid-1700s.

TRAVEL RESOURCES

Information about things to see and do in Oxford is available from the **Oxford Business Association**.
- PortofOxford.com; 410.226.5122 (town offices)

As of this writing, the **Oxford-Bellevue Ferry** operates from April 15 into the fall months, with trips running about every 20 minutes between 9am and sunset. Please check for current hours before you go.
- OxfordBellevueFerry.com; 410.745.9023

More information about things to do and places to go in St. Michaels, Easton, Oxford, and other nearby towns is available from **Talbot County Tourism**. That office also has a helpful driving tour brochure listing sites associated with events in the life of Frederick Douglass.
- Talbot Visitor Center, 11 South Harrison Street, Easton, Maryland
- TourTalbot.org; 410.770.8000

24: An Unlikely Appeal for Mercy

Centreville, Maryland

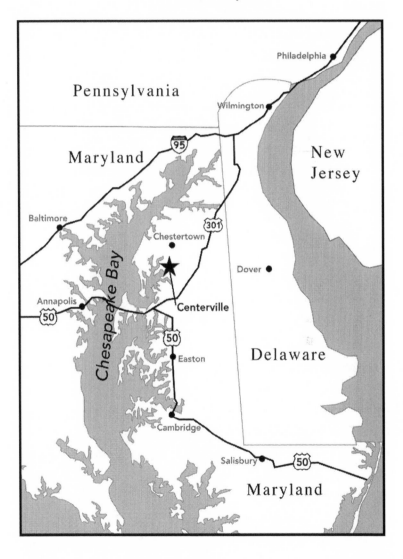

BIG PICTURE
That Stubborn Refusal

In the late 1970s, historians T.H. Breen and Steven Innes published a groundbreaking study of race relations in early colonial times on Virginia's Eastern Shore. Titled *Myne Owne Ground*, their book revealed a surprise about the early 1600s—it seems that there was a brief stretch of time in one small patch of the New World when some black men were treated in many ways as the equals of whites.

The records Breen and Innes pored through showed these free blacks owning large farms and participating fully in civic affairs. They were filing cases in court, winning judgements that showed no signs of prejudice, and receiving equal-looking treatment from merchants and others. This window of relatively equal opportunity for at least some blacks would close, of course, as the institution of slavery took hold across all of the Delmarva Peninsula.

One particular turn of phrase from *Myne Owne Ground* came to my mind when I was looking into the story that follows here. It appears at a point where Innes and Breen are discussing the big-picture preconceptions that historians bring to the study of race in days gone by.

[T]he closer we examine specific biracial communities, either in the present or the past, the more we discover that gross generalizations about race are misleading, if not altogether incorrect. We find ourselves confronted with too many exceptions, with blacks and whites who stubbornly refuse to behave as blacks and whites are supposed to behave.

STORY
An Unlikely Appeal for Mercy

The main route through downtown Centreville, Maryland is a divided affair that dovetails quite nicely with the subject of this book. One-way Commerce Street heads up to the north while the-other-way Liberty Street heads to the south. The courthouse that stands in between these two at Broadway is the oldest still in continuous use in Maryland, dating clear back to the 1790s.

It was standing, then, when Phoebe Myers was born a free woman in 1803. There is no information available about Myers's younger years, but by the time she reached her 40s, she had given birth to at least one child, a daughter named Ellenora. It's not clear who her husband might have been, how he fit into this picture, or whether he was a slave or a free man. What we know for sure about Myers is thin gruel—she spun wool to earn money, she was illiterate, and she stood five feet, six inches tall.

And there's this: In 1855, she was arrested on charges of helping seven members of two enslaved families in a failed escape attempt. Both families, the

Johnsons and the Tildens, belonged to a man named Richard Bennett Carmichael.

Unlike Myers, we know a lot about Carmichael. Born in 1807, he became a lawyer in his early 20s, then served as a state delegate and in the U.S. House of Representatives before becoming a judge. The 1840 census listed him as owning six slaves. In 1850, he owned seven. In 1860, he owned 18. He had at least seven children with his wife, Elizabeth.

Judge Carmichael was a passionate supporter of slavery before the Civil War and an equally passionate supporter of the South once war broke out. In fact, he would be charged with treason in 1862. His arrest in the Talbot County Courthouse in Easton became quite a cause célèbre after federal agents went way over the top while arresting him, pistol-whipping the judge and dragging him straight off of the bench in the middle of a court case.

He was imprisoned for six months after that in Baltimore, but in the end he was not formally charged with or tried for any crime.

Back to Phoebe Myers: On December 5, 1855, she was convicted in court on all seven charges of harboring the runaways who belonged to Carmichael. There is no indication in court records that Myers had ever been charged with or suspected of similar crimes in the past. But this one time proved quite enough for the judge hearing the case. He sentenced Myers to prison for roughly six years apiece on each and every one of the seven charges—a breathtaking total of 42 years and six months. She entered the penitentiary in Baltimore on December 20, 1855, as prisoner number 4967.

Now here's the strange twist to this story, the one that brought to mind that phrase by Innes and Breen about people in the past who "stubbornly refuse" to play the roles we expect them to play. A couple of months after Myers landed in the penitentiary, Maryland Governor Thomas Watkins Ligon received a formal request that he pardon Phoebe Myers and allow her to be released immediately.

This petition was not the work of some do-gooder abolitionist. Rather, it came from none other than Richard Bennett Carmichael, the very slave owner whose human "property" had tried to run off with help from Myers. Several other prominent, slave-owning white residents of Centreville signed on to the petition as well.

Why would a man like Carmichael go out of his way to help a woman like Phoebe Myers? That is a mystery. There doesn't seem to be an old letter or diary entry in which he lays out his thinking, or at least no such item has turned up yet. All we know is that his surprising plea for mercy on behalf of Phoebe Myers was successful. She was released from prison on May 6, 1856, after serving less than five months of that 42-year sentence. As far as I can tell, no one knows what became of her after she walked out of that jail.

TRAVEL RESOURCES

Downtown Centreville has a good number of shops, galleries, and restaurants. Information about things to do and see here and in surrounding towns is available from **Queen Anne's County Tourism**.

- Queen Anne's Visitor Center, 425 Piney Narrows Road, Chester, Maryland
- VisitQueenAnnes.com; 410.604.2100

The Queen Anne's County Visitor Center above is actually about 20 miles from Centreville. Two other such centers are closer. The **Kent County Visitor Center** in Chestertown is 15 miles to the north.

- 122 North Cross Street, Chestertown, Maryland

The state runs a **Maryland Welcome Center** that is about five miles to the northeast, along Route 301.

- 1000 Welcome Center Drive, Centreville, Maryland

25: THE OTHER HARRIET'S WILD RIDE FOR FREEDOM

Chestertown, Maryland

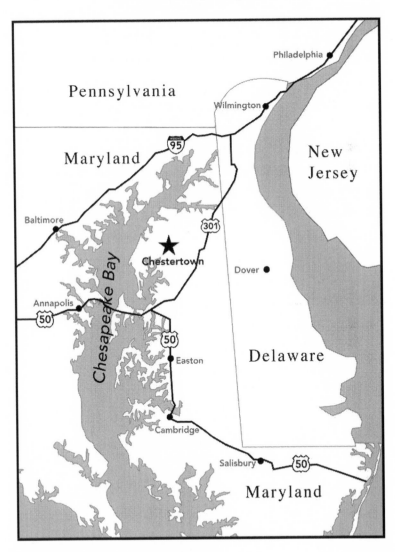

BIG PICTURE
A Ride for the Ages

American history has its share of famous horseback rides. There is the "Midnight Ride" of Paul Revere, of course, in which the Massachusetts patriot spread the news that the British army was on the move. Then there is Delaware's Caesar Rodney, who made a mad dash to Philadelphia so as to cast the last-minute vote that put Delaware in support of the Declaration of Independence on July 4, 1776.

If things worked a little differently in the field of history, the name of Harriet Shephard might rank on that level in the annals of the Underground Railroad. But alas, the stories we end up hearing about depend on what survives over the centuries. There are no old records, letters, account books, or court cases that have much to say about this other Harriet from the Eastern Shore of Maryland. When was she born? When did she die? Who was she married to? And what happened to her after she made her mad dash out of bondage?

STORY
The Other Harriet's Wild Ride for Freedom

What we do know is Harriet Shephard was born into slavery somewhere in the town of Chestertown in Kent County, Maryland. We can be kinda sorta sure that her owner there was a man named George W.T. Perkins, since the census records listing the first names of Perkins's slaves are a pretty close match with the names of Harriet and her children.

By 1855 Harriet had given birth to five children, ranging in age from newborn to about 12. Their names were Anna Maria, Edwin, Eliza Jane, Mary Ann, and John Henry.

The town those children grew up in was already thick with history. Today, Chestertown ranks as the colonial king of the Eastern Shore, as more buildings from that pre-independence era are still standing here than anywhere else in the state outside of Annapolis. There is no historic marker or specific site here that will put you in touch with the story of the Shephard family, but the sights you'll see while strolling the town today include a good number of buildings that Harriet and her children likely walked past as well.

There seems to have been something contagious about escapes along the Underground Railroad. They came in batches, as if some runaway fever were making the rounds. I've touched elsewhere in these pages on the rash of runaways that had Harriet Tubman's home turf of Dorchester County in such an uproar in the spring of 1857.

The fall of 1855 was like that here in Chestertown. One group of 10 slaves made their escape in September. Another group of seven fled on October 20.

Harriet Shephard caught the fever on October 26, a Friday. We have only vague hints as to why she ran. The Underground Railroad chronicler William Still met

Harriet during her escape and later recalled her saying that she had not received "kind treatment" from her master. Still also praised Harriet for a strong desire to see her children grow up free of slavery.

Harriet's ride was a remarkable affair, even by the standards of the Underground Railroad. Not many women led their own escapes in the manner of these two Harriets, Tubman and Shephard. And there may not be any comparable case at all in which that woman was the mother of five, with all of her children in tow.

In all, there were 11 people in Harriet Shephard's party. Seven were minors—Harriet's five children and two enslaved teenagers, William Thomas Freeman and Thomas Jervis Gooseberry. We do not know the names of the other three, though two of them were reportedly an aunt and an uncle of Harriet's.

Another remarkable element of this escape is its sheer brazenness. At some point in the afternoon or evening of that Friday, Harriet and her makeshift band of runaways simply absconded with two carriages and several horses from Harriet's master.

Most of the other escape stories in this book are secretive affairs involving nighttime travel, hopscotching from one hideaway to another. Harriet and her runaways didn't do that—they just ran, flat out and as fast as they could. While you stroll the streets of Chestertown today, put an image in your mind's eye of that carriage and those horses flying by.

Harriet must have pushed those stolen horses to the limits of their endurance, considering that her party of

11 rolled into Wilmington, Delaware, 45 miles away, the next morning. She was there almost before the white folks back home had a chance to notice she was gone.

"It is but reasonable to suppose that the first report [of this escape in Chestertown] must have produced a shock scarcely less stunning than an earthquake...," Still would write in his journal a few weeks later, adding a bit of speculation about the "cursings and threatenings" that likely filled the air in town when the news broke.

Harriet and her compatriots don't seem to have had much in the way of a plan beyond running those horses as hard as they could. It's probably safe to assume that they took the straightest possible route to Wilmington. The modern-day Route 301 is one candidate, though perhaps some other road ran along a parallel route back then.

Once in Wilmington, the 11 runaways made no effort to disguise themselves. They simply "ventured up into the heart of town in carriages, looking as innocent as if they were going to meeting to hear an old-fashioned Southern sermon," Still reported.

But luck was on Harriet's side. One or more sympathetic souls spied her party's arrival and guessed their predicament. They got word to Underground Railroad conductor Thomas Garrett, who soon advised the runaways to simply abandon those horses and carriages right in the middle of the street.

Slave hunters arrived on the scene a few hours later, on Saturday afternoon. They found the stolen horses right away, but Harriet and her crew were another matter. By then, Garrett had the runaways in disguises and on their way north via a string of safe houses in southern Pennsylvania, first in Longwood and then in Pocopson and then in Kimberton. It was early November by the time Harriet and her children arrived in the Philadelphia office of William Still.

We don't know what happened after that. The historians who've looked at the flight of Harriet Shephard speculate that she and her children were transported into upstate New York and on across the Canadian border, but no one knows for sure where they landed, or what became of them later in life.

The only fleeting mention of Harriet that appears in the historical record after her mad dash to freedom is from back in Chestertown. There, a notation in the Maryland census records from 1860 shows Harriet's former owner reporting to the government that several of his slaves belonged in an official category called "fugitives from the state."

In other words, they were still free.

BONUS STORY
Fortune Tellers and Perfidious Scamps

I have not come across an estimate of how many slaves escaped from Chestertown and Kent County in the years after Harriet Shephard's ride to freedom, but the numbers must have been significant.

In 1858, slave owners were once again up in arms over the matter of runaways. This time, they were taking the law into their own hands in a desperate, violent campaign to prevent any more of their "property" from running off.

On June 23 of that year, a stranger approached the house of James Bowers, a white, anti-slavery Quaker who had been acquitted a couple of years before on charges of aiding a runaway. That stranger asked Bowers for help with a broken-down carriage and then led him into an ambush by a group of 30 men. Bowers was soon dragged into some nearby woods, where he was tarred and feathered and then told to leave the state immediately, or else.

Bowers was forced to leave his pregnant wife behind that day. The local press branded him a "perfidious scamp" and an "evil doer." Despite this public disparagement, Bowers returned to Kent County after the Civil War, moving onto a piece of property near the modern-day town of Worton. He is buried in a Quaker cemetery near the town of Lynch.

In the days after the Bowers ambush, Kent County's proslavery vigilantes went after another target, a free black woman named Harriet Tillison. This woman apparently had a habit of wandering the backroads of Kent and Cecil counties, where she had earned a reputation for her skills in "conjuration and fortune telling."

According to a local newspaper account, however, Tillison's various comings and goings were often suspiciously "followed by the escape of slaves." That same article describes her as "dwarfish in appearance, scarcely weighing 50 pounds," and perhaps quite light-skinned, as if she "has a strong infusion of the Anglo-Saxon."

This is tantalizing stuff: Was she, perhaps, a Tubman-style conductor operating on the Upper Eastern Shore? Alas, there is nothing else in the way of surviving evidence about her. All we know is that Tillison, too, was tarred and feathered by that mob. There is no definitive record of what became of her after that.

TRAVEL RESOURCES

Downtown Chestertown is full of shops, restaurants, parks, and other amenities. Information for visitors is available from the **Downtown Chestertown Association**.

- DowntownChestertown.org

Information about things to do both in Chestertown and throughout Kent County is available from **Kent County Tourism**.

- Kent County Visitor Center, 122 North Cross Street, Chestertown, Maryland
- KentCounty.com/visitors; 410.778.0416

26: 'We All Knelt Down on the Snow-Covered Ground'

Galena, Maryland

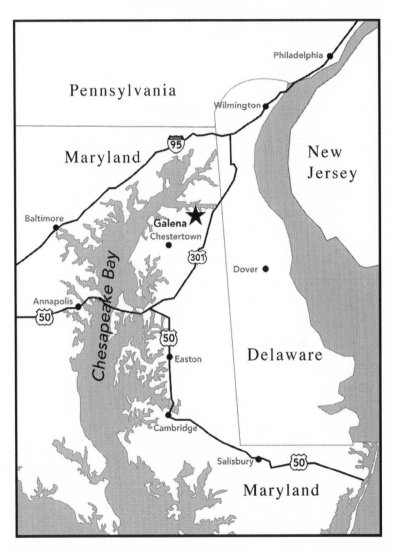

BIG PICTURE
Where Slavery Meets Sadism

If a movie ever gets made about the life of Isaac Mason, it would need to be done by a director who comes to the project half-crazy to begin with—Quentin Tarantino say, or better yet, one of those twisted South Korean directors who are always shifting from sadistic horror to slapstick comedy in the blink of an eye.

At times, the stories that Mason tells in his autobiography are quite excruciating. His journey, like so many others along the Underground Railroad, started from a place of powerlessness. Usually, the situations that sparked slaves to make a run for freedom had some semblance of logic about them. A farmer in need of money decides to sell his "property" at the auction block. An overseer determined to keep his charges in line relies too heavily on the whip.

Isaac Mason's story is in another category of powerlessness altogether, one that is all the more surreal and terrifying for the sheer randomness of its violence.

STORY
'We All Knelt Down on the Snow-Covered Ground'

Mason was born in 1822 in the town of George Town Cross Roads, on Maryland's Upper Eastern Shore.

Today, that town is called Galena. It had 500 residents in Mason's day. It has 600 residents now.

The town is just off Route 301, the pretty four-lane highway that runs between Kent Island in Maryland and Wilmington in Delaware. Downtown Galena is a tiny, quiet affair, but interesting. There are a couple of places to enjoy down-home food, a couple of antiques shops, and an interesting grocery store that specializes in healthy foods.

North of town, Main Street changes its name to Augustine Herman Highway en route to the town of Georgetown, on the Sassafras River. That's the direction you'll find Toal Park on the right-hand side, a little way outside of Galena. The entrance to the park is a nondescript affair; it looks like a facility that will be of interest only to the families of Little League kids, but if you drive all the way to the tree line in back, you will find your way to a hilly little stroll through some woods with intermittent water views—a perfect setting for giving some thought to days gone by and the strange saga of Isaac Mason.

He was the oldest of five siblings. His enslaved mother, Sophia, worked as a housemaid for her owner, a widow named Hannah Woodland. His free father, Zekiel, helped run the Woodland family farm. All seems to have been relatively calm with Isaac's young life until the age of 13, at which point Hannah Woodland passed away.

In time, her estate sold the farm (and young Isaac, and his mother) to a man named Isaac Taylor.

Somewhere in the transition, Mason's family watched one of its elders endure a casual bit of cruelty that was all too common in slavery times:

> My grandfather, in consideration of his old age and the time being past for useful labor, was handsomely rewarded with his freedom, an old horse called the "old bay horse"—which was also past the stage of usefulness—and an old cart; but, alas! no home to live in or a place to shelter his head from the storm.

This new owner rented the teenaged Isaac out to a family with the name of Hyde. All went reasonably well there until the day when Isaac returned from a rabbit-hunting expedition with friends and entered the kitchen on one of his routine chores, fetching a milk pail.

For no apparent reason, Mrs. Hyde locked the kitchen door behind him and ordered him to remove some of his clothing. Then she commenced whipping him with "well roasted hickory wottels." Mason endured it for a time, but then resisted, pushing Mrs. Hyde aside and jumping out a window.

He hid out for a while, first with his mother and then with the aforementioned grandfather. When things calmed down and Mason was able to show his face again, he was rented out to a different family, the Wallises. They in turn assigned him to work for a cabinetmaker and casket-maker in nearby Chestertown, James Mansfield.

Mason promised this new master that he would be a good slave. Mr. Mansfield seemed pleased with his new hire.

> I got along for the first two weeks very nicely.... I concluded I was all right and was going to have a nice time at my new home. At this time there was not the dread of a daily whipping and the loss of one meal a day. It was not long before I was to learn that storms followed calms, and war came after peace.

One Friday morning about four weeks into his new assignment, Mason's new mistress, Mary Mansfield, approached and asked him what he was working on.

> [H]er face was awfully red; there was something wrong but I could not divine it. She hurriedly went out of the room where I was, into the back room, and got her cowhide; without the least ceremony she lit on me—the same as a hungry hawk on an innocent chicken.

Mason begged her to stop, but she kept at it even as blood streamed from his head and back. She relented only when she herself was overcome by exhaustion. Mason had no idea what, if anything, he had done wrong.

Then things got really weird. Mary Mansfield never raised a whip against Isaac again. Instead, she demanded that her husband do the deed on a regular basis while she watched. James Mansfield did not have a reputation as a gentle sort of slave owner, but the sick nature of this ritual proved too much even for him. Mason overheard James tell his wife one day that that "he would not do it any more to gratify her."

Mansfield eventually moved young Mason away from his home, and from Mrs. Mansfield. He assigned Isaac to work on farmland outside of town and had him work as well on the casket-making end of his business, transporting dead bodies to cemeteries.

> On one occasion I went to bury the wife of a high sheriff, and to my surprise and confusion found that all the men were drunk. When they arrived at the burying ground they were just fit for business—not to bury, but to quarrel.

Those men proceeded to drop the casket while pulling it off of the wagon that served as a hearse. See what I mean about the need for a little slapstick comedy in the midst of that potential horror movie about Mason's time in slavery? Not knowing what would happen next, Mason fled the scene and returned to the Mansfield farm.

He worked five years on that farm and never once got whipped. While on a business trip with his master to Baltimore, however, Mason found himself alone with a bit of free time and decided to walk the streets of the city. Two white strangers beat him savagely for the offense of walking between them on a sidewalk instead of circling around them by way of the street. Even Mason's master had no idea that this rule existed in the city.

Back in Kent County, things went completely off the rails. When Mary Mansfield gave birth to a child, a neighbor came calling to mark the occasion and help out with chores. Mason was back at the house on this day, and so he was there when this woman served plates full of rotten meat to the slaves. Mason gave his share to some dogs.

Seeing this, the woman decided that it was some sort of terrible offense against her. She demanded that Mason be punished. James Mansfield began beating Mason with a stick. The slave fought back, pushing his master over a pile of wood. Mansfield called for his gun. Mason fled, leaping over one fence and making his way toward a second one.

> As I ascended the second fence ... he aimed his gun, firing three shots at me. The first shot grazed my head, removing a little hair; the second touched my ear, and the third passed through my hat; but they did not stop me from running.

Again, Isaac Mason went into hiding. Mansfield eventually sent word out through the grapevine of slaves and free blacks that everything would be fine if he returned to the farm. He did, but things were not fine at all. The woman who had served up that rotten meat was a member of the Wallis family, which was renting Mason out to the Mansfields. Her father, Hugh Wallis, saw Mason one day and commenced, out of the blue, beating him with a pitchfork.

It was around this time that Mason heard rumors that he was about to be sold to a slave trader from New Orleans. He decided that he had no choice but to run. He talked two fellow slaves into joining him on the journey.

Mason planned his escape carefully, working out the details during a meeting with a free black Underground Railroad conductor in George Town Cross Roads named Joe Brown. They set a rendezvous for Brown's cabin one night the following week. The price of transit would be $9. But this is what Mason and his compatriots found when they showed up at Brown's house at the appointed time:

> To the horror of all we found Joe lying on the floor dead drunk. Joshua and George did not know Brown's failings; they became alarmed at the situation and talked strongly about going back home.

Mason convinced his companions to stick it out for one more day. Mason's mother lived nearby. The trio hid in the attic at her place until Brown emerged from his stupor the next afternoon. Snow covered the ground when they set out that evening on the walk to Wilmington, Delaware, 35 miles away.

They got within eight miles of their destination when Brown called the march to a halt. He told his passengers to hide in a wooded area and wait for him to return and fetch them. In the woods, the trio found a seemingly perfect bit of shelter, a gigantic white oak that had fallen to the ground so recently that it was still full of foliage.

Shortly after daybreak, Mason found himself enduring another round of slapstick comedy. He and his friends heard the baying of fox-hounds in the distance. As that sound grew closer, they spied a party of white hunters on horseback, riding in after the hounds. The fox that those hounds were trailing was desperate to return to the safety of its home.

> To my great astonishment, I discovered that we were lying over the hole that led to the reynard's den. He made two or three attempts to get into the hole but we succeeded in beating him off.

The hunters stayed in the vicinity for much of the day, but somehow never discovered the runaways. When darkness came at last, Mason decided to give up on his missing conductor, who had been gone almost a whole day by this point. Mason located the North Star up in the sky, remembering how an old man had once told him that the "Lord had placed it there to lead people out of slavery."

Five miles into this leg of their journey, they ran smack dab into Joe Brown. He gave the famished runaways some food, then handed them off to an elderly man Mason had never seen before.

> There are a great many venturesome things a man will do, when determined to escape from danger or an evil, that he would not do when otherwise situated. To think that we had placed our fate in the hands of a man who was, to us, an utter stranger. ... The experience of the past had taught us the lesson to trust and go forward, and forward we went.

Mason had lost track of what month it was, but he kept up with the days of the week. He knew that it was a Tuesday "when our eyes rested on [the state of Pennsylvania,] where liberty for the negro slave could be enjoyed." Mason asked that stranger of a conductor if it would be all right to pause there and say a prayer.

> The old man readily consented to the proposal, and we all knelt down on the snow-covered ground and offered up humble thanksgiving, and petitions for future protection and guidance, to the Great Supreme Ruler of heaven and earth.

Amen, Mr. Mason.

POSTCRIPT
A 'Premature Graveyard'

Even in freedom, Isaac Mason continued to endure one close call after another. He initially settled on a farm in Pennsylvania, where he met a woman he planned to marry. Those plans were put on hold, however, when slave catchers from his native Kent County appeared in the area and kidnapped another former slave from a neighboring farm.

Mason went back on the run at that point. He did marry that woman eventually, and they settled in Philadelphia. But then, in another turn of slapstick coincidence, he crossed paths one day with a member of the dreaded Wallis family and ended up on the run yet again. He went to Boston this time, and then joined the larger black exodus to Canada that greeted the passage of the Fugitive Slave Act of 1850.

A decade later, Mason signed on to join a group of blacks who had been recruited to leave the country and establish a new settlement on the island of Haiti. He had high hopes at the time of his departure, but nearly died in the storms his ship encountered en route. His experiences on the island amounted to nothing but disaster and disappointment. In the end, he came to regard the whole scheme to encourage the emigration of blacks out of the country as nothing but a "premature graveyard."

He finally ended up in Worcester, Massachusetts. It was there, he decided, that "I should dwell until the end of my days." He was in his 70s when he published his memoir. No one seems to know for sure when he died. I hope and trust that he passed away in the comfort of the home he had found at long last.

TRAVEL RESOURCES

Galena is in Kent County, as is the nearby town of Georgetown. Information about things to do in both of those towns as well as the surrounding countryside is available from **Kent County Tourism**.

- Kent County Visitor Center, 122 North Cross Street, Chestertown, Maryland
- KentCounty.com/visitors; 410.778.0416

27: LOVE COMES IN A BOX

Chesapeake City, Maryland

BIG PICTURE
The Straight Shot to Philly

Before 1829, boats bound for Philadelphia from the Chesapeake Bay had to take the roundabout route, sailing down to the mouth of the Bay and then circling back up along the Atlantic Coast, into the Delaware Bay, and, finally, up the Delaware River.

The opening of the Chesapeake & Delaware Canal that year on the upper reaches of the Delmarva Peninsula made things much easier. A 14-mile straight shot between the Elk River on the west and the Delaware River on the east, the C&D Canal slashed some 300 nautical miles and 15 hours of time off a trip between Baltimore and Philadelphia.

Those savings diminished from points farther south, of course, but the canal route had a couple of other things going for it. The Chesapeake Bay had lots of sheltered harbors to offer in bad weather, so it was a safer sail. It also had more ports of call, with each one offering boat captains the possibility of extra profits by way of deliveries and pickups.

Quite a few boats taking this new route across the upper Delmarva Peninsula had passengers aboard as well. Some of those passengers were slaves trying to find a way to freedom.

STORY
Love Comes in a Box

Back in 1850, William Adams fell head over heels for one gritty young girl. A free black barber in Baltimore who also worked shucking oysters in the city's taverns, he was a soft-spoken young man with a four-inch scar running up his cheek from a corner of his mouth. There is no telling how he came by this mark of distinction.

The object of his affections was Lear Green, a pretty, round-faced girl of 18 who was blessed with what one man who met her described as "a peculiar modesty and grace." She was a slave, owned by a butter merchant in the East Baltimore neighborhood of Old Town.

Adams proposed. Green said no. It wasn't that she didn't love him. Rather, she had decided not to bear any children into bondage. With the status of slaves passing through mothers in those days, she simply wasn't going to marry anyone, at least not while enslaved.

This would have been the end for most affairs, but Adams seems to have been a man of uncommon determination. He soon asked his mother to come down from New York City and run point on an escape that should be much more famous than it is.

One good place to stop and think about Lear Green's voyage to freedom is in Chesapeake City, a pretty town of 700 in Cecil County, Maryland. It's home to the C&D Canal Museum if you're interested in the workings and history of the waterway. The last time my wife and I were up this way, we brought along bikes and rode a stretch of the first-rate strolling/cycling path that runs along the north bank of the canal between Chesapeake City and Delaware City, another pretty little town that's well worth a visit.

Upon arriving in Baltimore, William Adams's mother bought a ticket aboard a steamship for Philadelphia. Among the bags she checked that day was an old sailor's chest with Lear Green curled up inside. I haven't come across an account that includes a first name for this Mrs. Adams, but I can say that she was putting her own freedom at risk. Free blacks who got caught aiding runaways were sometimes sentenced to be sold into slavery for the rest of their lives.

At this point, the business of the ships running through the canal was focused primarily on cargo. Passengers like Mrs. Adams were an afterthought. She didn't have a stateroom, or even an assigned seat. She had something more like a general admission pass to the deck, which put her right in the midst of all that cargo.

During the night, Mrs. Adams found her way to the crate that held her wannabe daughter-in-law at least once and perhaps twice. She untied the ropes binding the box closed and lifted the lid to let in a little fresh air and "see if the poor child still lived."

There is no surviving account from Lear Green herself about what it was like being cooped up in that chest. But we can get a sense for her ordeal through a man who made the same sort of journey through this same canal aboard the same sort of ship nine years later, in 1859.

William Peel's journey to freedom began in Baltimore, too. The 25-year-old was enslaved by Robert H. Carr, a grocery store owner who had gotten into the habit of selling off slaves like so many bags of flour. Convinced that he would be the next one to go, Peel asked a free black friend to pack him in a box and put him on a steamship to Philadelphia.

The first misfortune that struck Peel during that journey was an excruciating cramp. It was so painful that he "had his faith taxed to the utmost—indeed was brought to the very verge of 'screaming aloud' ere relief came."

After the cramp passed, "faintness" and "exhaustion" came over him in such a wave that he feared he was about to die. When Peel finally came out of that haze, a third trial arrived, this one a "cold chill" that seemed "to freeze the very blood in his veins and gave him intense agony."

Peel's voyage took 17 hours. Lear Green's ordeal lasted 18.

Once in Philadelphia, the sailor's chest where Green was curled up got loaded onto a carriage and taken to the home of a friend of Mrs. Adams. Someone involved in this plot had managed to make the right connections by this point, because the crate was then forwarded via another carriage to William Still at the office at the American Anti-Slavery Society. There, at long last, the 18-year-old emerged.

Such hungering and thirsting for liberty, as was evinced by Lear Green, made the efforts of the most ardent friends, who were in the habit of aiding fugitives, seem feeble in the extreme. Of all the heroes in Canada, or out of it, who have purchased their liberty by downright bravery, through perils the most hazardous, none deserve more praise than Lear Green.

Lear stayed with Still for several days, until she had recovered enough from her ordeal to travel north to meet Adams. The couple did indeed get married, settling in the town of Elmira, New York.

I wish I could report that Lear and William enjoyed a long, fruitful marriage, but alas, Lear passed away three years later at the age of 21. The cause is unknown. The mother-in-law who risked everything to bring Lear north also died at about the same time. I haven't come across any reports about what became of Adams in the years after that.

As for William Still, the brief encounter he had with this trio made quite an impression on him. When he published a book-length version of his journals recounting meetings with hundreds of different runaways over the years, he singled out Lear Green as someone with "a strong claim to a high place among the heroic women of the nineteenth century." He even kept the chest that carried her along the C&D Canal as a keepsake of that heroism.

BONUS STORY
Captains Courageous

Do you remember John Bowley, the free black man who rescued his wife and two children from the auction block in Cambridge, Maryland? He eventually sailed the family up to Baltimore, where they met up with Harriet Tubman, who then led them overland across the border and into Pennsylvania.

The most likely reason Tubman and Bowley chose that roundabout route over a straight sailing shot to Philadelphia through the C&D Canal is the way vessels would come under scrutiny at the four locks on the canal. A boat full of blacks on the run was bound to raise suspicions at those locks.

For a white captain, however, things were different. At least two such men carried runaways along this canal during the 1850s. William Still referred to them as "Captain B" and "Captain F," but historians have cracked that code. William Baylis sailed his schooner, the *Keziah*, out of Norfolk. Albert Fountain hailed from Baltimore, and his schooner was called the *City of Richmond*.

Both were veteran seamen with the mix of experience and wits needed to manage a high-risk operation. In the summer of 1856, Baylis was very nearly busted at a lock on the canal while 15 runaways were hiding aboard the *Keziah* in a false-bottom compartment. Authorities investigating an escape in Norfolk had sent a message by telegraph, asking colleagues up near the canal to keep an eye out for Baylis.

Three investigators came aboard, taking statements from Baylis and two of his crew members. In the midst of these official conversations, Baylis managed to make sure the authorities overheard he and his sailors small talking about how "the yellow fever had been raging very bad in Norfolk." The investigators left the boat without conducting a proper search.

Fountain pulled a similarly gutsy trick one time aboard the *City of Richmond*. He was getting ready to leave Norfolk with 21 runaways aboard when authorities descended on his vessel, demanding to inspect it. Feigning outraged innocence, Fountain grabbed an axe and began furiously splintering deck logs, vowing to chop his boat to smithereens if that's what it would take to prove his innocence. Those investigators backed down, too.

Fountain and Baylis were regulars when it came to delivering escaped slaves to William Still in Philadelphia. Both charged runaways for their services, though it's unclear how much of those payments were about covering expenses and how much might have been a matter of profit for captains and crew.

Baylis would eventually get arrested, convicted, and sentenced to 40 years in prison for his part in this Underground Railroad work, though he served only a small fraction of that time before getting pardoned.

I am not sure if Fountain ever got caught. I do know that he earned a reputation through the years for delivering "human cargo" of the highest order. Here is what William Still had to say about that:

> Captain F. was not ... in the habit of bringing numbskulls; indeed, he brought none but the bravest and most intelligent.

Baylis and Fountain were both sailing with runaways hidden aboard during an incredible deep freeze that descended on the Chesapeake Bay in the winter of 1855-56. The *Cecil Whig* reported that February that "the ice on the Elk river about Courthouse Point is from 15 to 18 inches thick." That point sits right along the only route into the canal from the Bay.

They had both sailed out of Norfolk on this particular trip. Still reports that they departed in mid-January, but, incredibly, didn't arrive in Philadelphia until March 20.

> The sufferings for food, which [the fugitives on these boats] were called upon to endure, were beyond description.

The arrivals recovered quickly from their frozen ordeal, however, with volunteers in Still's office feeding them well for a few days and arranging to get them all outfitted in new clothes. By the time they set out on the next leg of their journey to freedom, "they looked more like a pleasuring party than like fugitives."

CONNECTIONS

- The story mentioned here about John Bowley rescuing his wife and children from the auction block in Cambridge and then sailing up the Chesapeake Bay is in Chapter 2.
- The Postscript to Chapter 12 includes a discussion by Underground Railroad chronicler William Still on the issue of Captain Baylis charging runaways for his services.

TRAVEL RESOURCES

Information about shops, restaurants, and things to do in Chesapeake City is available from the **Chesapeake City Chamber of Commerce**.

- ChesapeakeCity.com; 800.757.6030

Information about things to do and see nearby in other towns and parks in the area is available from **Cecil County Tourism**.

- SeeCecil.org; 410.996.6299

If you want to see the **C&D Canal Museum**, be sure to call in advance and double-check on the hours that are posted online. I tried to visit a couple of times without doing that, only to find the gate closed.

- 815 Bethel Road, Chesapeake City, Maryland

- ChesapeakeCity.com/cd-canal-museum/;
  410.855.5621

The Maryland section of the strolling and cycling trail that runs along the canal is called the **Ben Cardin Trail**. The Delaware section is called the **Michael Castle Trail**.

- Maryland: ChesapeakeCity.com/cd-canal-recreational-trail/
- Delaware: EcoDelaware.com/places.php

If you choose to visit Delaware City, too, while in this area, information is available from the **Greater Wilmington Convention & Visitors Bureau**.

- VisitWilmingtonDE.com/listings/delaware-city-historic-district/111/; 800.489.6664

28: Fred Bailey Finally Finds His Way to Freedom

Havre de Grace, Maryland

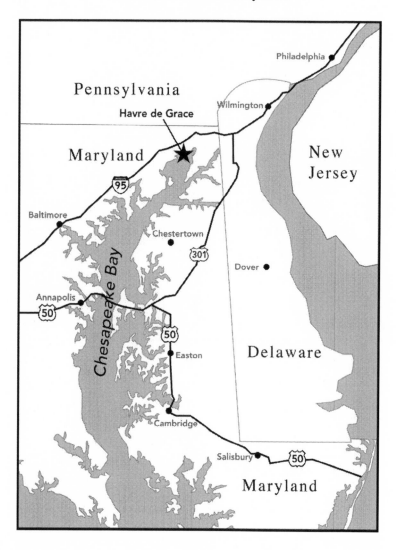

BIG PICTURE
The Times They Were a Changin'

In slavery, Frederick Douglass was known as Fred Bailey. The story of young Fred's second run for freedom starts back in Talbot County, on the Eastern Shore of Maryland. That's where Fred had plotted his first escape attempt with a group of friends, only to get betrayed and land instead in the Easton jail.

In the wake of that failure, Fred's owner, Thomas Auld, sent Fred to Baltimore to live with and work for Auld's brother, Hugh, and Hugh's wife, Sophia. Fred had lived with this couple in Fells Point in his younger years, but the Baltimore he returned to at the age of 18 was a very different place from the one he knew back then.

During the five short years Fred had been away from Baltimore, the city had changed enormously. A gigantic wave of Irish immigration had led to a bitter, often violent rivalry over job opportunities, pitting these new white arrivals against the population of free and enslaved black locals. The tensions ran especially high in the shipyards of Fells Point, where trouble would find its way to Fred soon enough.

STORY
Fred Bailey Finally Finds His Way to Freedom

One day while Fred was on the job in a shipyard, a man named Edward North took a swing at him. North was the leader of a gaggle of white men who were always talking about how the "niggers" were trying "to take the country" and "ought to be killed."

Though still in his teens, Fred Bailey had reached a place in life where he wasn't afraid to defend himself, despite his lowly legal status as a slave. He promptly picked North up and threw him into the Patapsco River.

On another occasion Fred got into a dispute with a white coworker over who did what wrong that caused a bolt to bend out of shape. One thing led to another, and soon, Fred was brawling with four white apprentices at the same time. A crowd of some 50 whites gathered around, many of them outraged by the sight of a black man swinging fists at white men.

> Kill him!—kill him!
> Kill the damned nigger!
> He struck a white person!
> Knock his brains out!

They pretty much did knock his brains out. When Fred got home, Sophia Auld took one look at his bloody face and burst into tears. Hugh Auld flew into a rage over the incident. He marched Fred down to the local Justice of the Peace on Bond Street, demanding the arrest of the men who had beaten up Fred. The Justice of the Peace did nothing.

After his failure in Easton, Fred had vowed that he would be better prepared to make a run at freedom the next time an opportunity presented itself. Whatever pennies he could set aside from his labors in the shipyards, he stashed away in a "Freedom Fund." He searched high and low for a set of forged or borrowed papers that might help him pass as a free man on ships and trains.

In the spring of 1838, Fred cut a deal with Hugh Auld in which he won a measure of freedom to be in charge of his own life. He would be able to hire himself out to shipyards on the condition that he pay Auld $3 at the end of every week. He would also be able to move out of Auld's house and into a place of his own, as long as he paid for everything out of his own pocket.

It was during this time that Fred helped form a club called the East Baltimore Mental Improvement Society. Members engaged in debate contests and learned classical theology and philosophy. Fred was already showing signs of a gift for public speaking. He used to bring down the house at society meetings with his parodies of white preachers. He also took up playing the violin, a hobby that he would stick with for a lifetime.

It was at a Mental Improvement Society social event that Fred met a young woman named Anna Murray. Like Fred, she hailed from the banks of Tuckahoe Creek on the Eastern Shore. Unlike Fred, she was legally free, having been born one month after her mother received her manumission papers.

In time, Fred proposed to her. Anna said yes.

That August, Fred left Baltimore to spend a few days in the countryside at a religious camp meeting. He stayed longer than planned, then showed up one day late at Hugh Auld's house to fork over that weekly $3 fee. Fred didn't think this would be a big deal, but Hugh exploded in anger over his lapse. He ordered Fred to move back into his house. He also made a vaguely threatening comment about how Fred soon wouldn't have to "trouble himself about finding work."

Fred wasn't ready to run quite yet. He gave himself a deadline of three weeks. His fiancée, Anna, responded to this turn of events by selling a bed she owned and then giving the proceeds to Fred. She also contributed to his Freedom Fund out of her own savings.

By Monday, September 3, 1838, he was ready. He hadn't found the perfect "freeman's papers," but he had gotten his hands on some sailor's "protection papers" that might be good enough to get him on board a train in the guise of a merchant seaman.

When Fred showed up at the train station in Baltimore, he had his every step carefully mapped out. He was dressed to look like a free black sailor, wearing a tarpaulin hat and a red shirt with a black cravat tied up around his neck.

He chose not to buy a ticket in advance, fearing that an agent in a ticket window might have extra time to inspect his less-than-perfect papers. Instead, he had a black friend appear at the very last second with all of his luggage so that he would have an excuse for boarding the train in a last-second frenzy.

There were no Jim Crow laws back in slavery times. The car Fred hopped aboard was no doubt full of both blacks and whites. The moment Fred had been dreading arrived when a ticket taker appeared, making his way down the aisle.

The heart of no fox or deer, with hungry hounds on his trail, in full chase, could have beaten more anxiously or noisily than did mine.

By federal law, train companies back then could be held liable if they failed to take steps to identify runaway slaves. These laws worked in the same way as modern-day rules governing the sale of liquor and cigarettes to minors. The moment of truth arrived:

"I suppose you have your free papers."
"No sir, I never carry my free papers to sea."
"But you have something to show you are a free man, have you not?"
"Yes, sir! I have a paper with the American eagle on it that will carry me around the world!"

Fred tried to deliver his lines with a patriotic flourish. The conductor barely glanced at his papers, taking the money for his fare to Wilmington and then moving on.

This brings us to Havre de Grace, a postcard-pretty town that lies along the railroad route between Baltimore and Wilmington. Technically speaking, the town isn't on the Delmarva Peninsula at all, of course, but it does brush right up against the edge of the Eastern Shore. Including this "harbor of grace" as the destination for this chapter allows me to include a really important story in this book. Plus, it gives you the chance to spend some quality time in a town full of history and charm.

On the day Fred Bailey passed through in 1838, he was presumably too preoccupied to pay attention to his surroundings. The stately old Concord Point Lighthouse dates to 1827, so it was here that day. The light ran on whale oil back then. There are little museums you can visit while in town that are dedicated to maritime history, waterfowl hunting, and a canal that was under construction when Douglass passed through. It would open for business two years later, in 1840.

Do you remember those funny Southwest Airlines commercials in which one important moment in life or another goes horribly awry and the tagline is, "Wanna get away?" That's the sort of moment Fred Bailey endured here in Havre de Grace, where everyone had to get off the train and board a ferry that would take them across the Susquehanna River. There, they would board another train for the second leg of the journey.

In a dreadful coincidence, one of the workers on that ferry turned out to be an old acquaintance of Fred's—a black man named Nichols. To make matters worse, this man saw through Fred's disguise and proceeded to greet his old friend loudly, and by name. He asked Fred where he was going. He asked why in the world he was dressed up in such a silly sailor's costume.

> [Nichols] came very near to betraying me.... I got away from my old and inconvenient acquaintance as soon as I could decently do so, and went to another part of the boat.

Two more near misses followed that encounter. As he got ready to board his train car for the second leg of the journey to Wilmington, Fred looked up into the window of a train that had arrived at the ferry stop from the opposite direction and saw a supervisor at one of the shipyards where Fred worked. If that supervisor had looked out the window at that moment, he would have recognized Fred in an instant.

Then, once on board, Fred found himself sharing a car with another white man he recognized from the shipyards, a German blacksmith.

> [He] looked at me very intently, as if he thought he had seen me somewhere before in his travels. I really believe he knew me, but had no heart to betray me. At any rate, he saw me escaping and held his peace.

It's interesting to ponder how history might have changed if any one of those three close calls had taken a turn for the worse. But they didn't, of course, and once Fred made it through Havre de Grace, the rest of his journey was smooth sailing.

He reached New York City on September 4 and immediately sent word back to Anna in Baltimore. The two were married on September 15 in a ceremony officiated by another escaped slave, Rev. James Pennington. In New York, Fred and Anna chose to adopt the last name of Johnson. It was only after they settled in New Bedford, Massachusetts, that they decided instead on the last name of Douglass.

In the years that followed, after he had become a famous anti-slavery orator capable of drawing overflow crowds into churches and auditoriums all over the North, Frederick Douglass would sometimes step on stage and begin his remarks with these words:

> I appear before you this evening as a thief and a robber. I stole this head, these limbs, this body from my master and ran off with them.

TESTIMONY
'The Loneliness Overcame Me'

In the days after he made his way to freedom, Frederick Douglass found himself on an emotional roller-coaster ride that started at the peak of elation but soon descended into the depths of loneliness and uncertainty. Interestingly, the experience he describes in *Narrative of the Life of Frederick Douglass* echoes quite closely the emotional journey that Harriet Tubman would go through in the wake of her own run to freedom 11 years later. Here is Douglass:

> I have been frequently asked how I felt when I found myself in a free State. I have never been able to answer the question with any satisfaction to myself. It was a moment of the highest excitement I ever experienced.
>
> I suppose I felt as one may imagine the unarmed mariner to feel when he is rescued by a friendly man-of-war from the pursuit of a pirate. In writing to a dear friend, immediately after my arrival at New York, I said I felt like one who had escaped a den of hungry lions.
>
> This state of mind, however, very soon subsided; and I was again seized with a feeling of great insecurity and loneliness. I was yet liable to be taken back, and subjected to all the tortures of slavery.
>
> This in itself was enough to damp the ardor of my enthusiasm. But the loneliness overcame me. There I was in the midst of thousands, and yet a perfect stranger; without home and without friends, in the midst of thousands of my own brethren—children of a common Father, and yet I dared not to unfold to any one of them my sad condition.

I was afraid to speak to any one for fear of speaking to the wrong one.... The motto which I adopted when I started from slavery was this— "Trust no man!" I saw in every white man an enemy, and in almost every colored man cause for distrust. It was a most painful situation; and, to understand it, one must needs experience it, or imagine himself in similar circumstances.

CONNECTIONS

- The story of Fred Bailey's first, failed run for freedom—the one that landed him in the Easton jail—is in Chapter 21.
- The emotional roller-coaster ride that Harriet Tubman experienced in the wake of her run to freedom is described in Chapter 18.

TRAVEL RESOURCES

Information about things to do and places to go in Havre de Grace, Maryland is available from the **Havre de Grace Office of Tourism**.

- ExploreHavredeGrace.com; 800.851.7756

Information about things to do and places to go in the broader area of Harford County, Maryland is available from **Harford County Tourism**.

- VisitHarford.com; 410.838.7777

Baltimore is outside of the geographic scope of this book, but if you are inclined to explore the experiences Frederick Douglass had during his two stints living in the Fells Point neighborhood, the place to start is the **Frederick Douglass Isaac Myers Maritime Park**.

- 1417 Thames Street, Baltimore, Maryland
- LivingClassrooms.org (look under "Our Programs" and then "Public Programming"); 410.685.0295

29: The Flight of the Dover Eight

Dover, Delaware

BIG PICTURE
The Pressure Cooker of 1857

The lush expanse of Dover Green has a serene, timeless air about it today. Located at the heart of a celebrated national historic district that is chock full of buildings dating to the 1700s, it has lots of interesting stories to tell about the early days of our country.

Dover was a hotbed of revolutionary activity in the waning days of colonial rule. It was here that Delaware earned its nickname, becoming the very First State to ratify the Constitution. And it was here in the 1850s that eight runaway slaves managed a jailbreak that unfolded like something straight out of a Hollywood action movie.

The old jail building where all this happened is not standing today, alas. But it was located here at the Green, right next to the Old Statehouse building, which dates to the late 1700s. Many of the historic buildings nearby were also standing on the night the Dover Eight arrived from Dorchester County, Maryland. Even the "Green" itself was in place—the open space originated as an outdoor market with vendors, but it had been transformed into a park in 1846.

The story of the Dover Eight's escape from this jail went viral, at least in the 19th century sense of the term. It appeared in first one, then another, and then countless other newspapers up and down the Atlantic seaboard. Then it spread some more, soon reaching across the whole country.

Abolitionists up north celebrated the affair with great gusto. Slavery defenders down south were humiliated—and furious. On the Eastern Shore of Maryland, the publicity made a bad year for slave owners even worse. Bad weather in that spring of 1857 had put the growing season at risk. And the Dover Eight affair was not an isolated incident—it was just the most famous of the rash of escapes around this time.

At raucous public meetings in Dorchester County and elsewhere, Maryland slave owners demanded that public officials start doing more about "protecting the slave property." They demanded that the police go after anyone and everyone suspected of encouraging or helping runaways.

They also began keeping closer track of the whereabouts of their slaves—and those of their neighbors as well. Without a doubt, some of them decided to dole out a bit of rough and unofficial vigilante justice as well.

For Harriet Tubman, the dramatic events in Dover were a mixed bag. The work of a conductor had always been dangerous, of course, but the risks of getting captured, jailed, and even killed went up dramatically after the events in Dover.

She was happy for the freedom of so many of her old neighbors in slavery, of course—as we shall see, she may even have provided them with some advice. But she also had more work to do. Her sister Rachel remained in bondage, as did Rachel's children. And then, a little later in the year, Tubman would receive another of those gifts that God was always sending her—this time, a presentiment that her parents might be in danger.

How much risk could she take on in order to bring her family members to freedom? That question grew more difficult after the sensational events in this story.

STORY
The Flight of the Dover Eight

No one knows for sure why Thomas Elliott and Denard Hughes picked the day of March 8, 1857 to make their run from the farm of Pritchett Meredith in Bucktown, Maryland. Later, Hughes would refer to Meredith as the "hardest man around," so it's easy to speculate about the beatings and whippings they may have endured.

But the decision to run wasn't a rash one made in the heat of a moment—it came only after careful planning. Some historians have speculated that Elliott, Hughes, and the six other Bucktown-area slaves who joined them on the run might have been working with instructions received along the Underground Railroad grapevine from Harriet Tubman herself.

Tubman, remember, spent much of her childhood in Bucktown. The store where she defied an overseer as a young girl and nearly died after getting hit in the head with a two-pound weight was within sight of the Meredith farmhouse. Tubman may well have been acquainted with some members of the Dover Eight, or at least with some of their relatives.

The group set off well-armed with knives and guns. They most likely stayed on overland routes, probably stopping at the East New Market home of a free black preacher, Samuel Green, and perhaps also at the cabin of Tubman's parents on Poplar Neck, near Preston.

Pritchett Meredith posted a $600 reward for his two slaves. Add in the prizes offered on the other six and the group's capture was worth a cool $3,000. That number proved too tempting for Thomas Otwell, a free black man who had earned Tubman's trust in the past with his work as an Underground Railroad operative. Otwell lived near Milford, in Southern Delaware, where he had recently started renting property from a white man with the last name of Hollis.

The two of them cooked up a scheme to betray the fleeing slaves and walk off with the reward money. Instead of leading the slaves to the next station on their journey to freedom, Otwell took them under cover of night straight into the Dover jail, where he left them in Hollis's hands.

But there was a problem. Otwell had arrived later than expected. The Dover sheriff, a man named Green, was supposed to be on hand when they got there, ready to spring the trap and lock the fugitives behind bars. But Green had given up on Otwell at 2am, heading into his nearby family quarters to get a bit of sleep.

When Otwell arrived at 4am, Hollis tried to coax the slaves into a room where he could lock them up, but one of the fleeing slaves, Henry Predeaux, pointed out in the moonlight of a clear night how the windows in the room were reinforced with iron bars. The runaways stayed in a hallway, growing more suspicious by the minute.

Sheriff Green finally appeared, but he, too, was unable to coax the slaves out of the hallway. He then hurried back to his living quarters in order to retrieve his gun. The slaves followed him right into those living quarters.

There, Predeaux sprang into action, throwing a shovel full of hot coals from the fireplace all over the room and onto a bed. He used a fireplace poker to break out a window, and then he kept the sheriff and Hollis at bay while his compatriots climbed out the window and dropped 12 feet onto the ground outside.

Finally, Predeaux pushed the sheriff away and made a run for the window himself. The sheriff's pistol jammed, and Predeaux, too, made it out of the building. Everyone else was gone by the time his feet hit the ground, so he set out to make his way to Wilmington and the home of famed Underground Railroad conductor Thomas Garrett.

That's a journey of 50 miles. Predeaux would soon become the first of the Dover Eight to reach freedom.

Six of the others had backtracked, returning along the route that had brought them to Dover. There, they overtook Thomas Otwell and soon were threatening to kill him. Otwell begged for his life. He vowed to get them back on track at the next Underground Railroad stop. Hearing this story later, conductor Thomas Garrett would observe,

It is a wonder that they acted with so much coolness and discretion. One of the men told me he would have killed [Otwell] at once had he not thought, if he did do it, he would have less chance to escape than if they committed no act of violence, which no doubt was a correct view.

The six ended up in the town of Willow Grove, Delaware. From there, they made their way along forested back roads, eventually reaching the Wilmington area, where Garrett's men managed to find them before the police did. They, too, soon reached freedom in Philadelphia.

The last of the eight to find freedom was Lavinia Woolfley. Sometime after making the leap from the jailhouse window, she had become separated from her husband James and the others. She managed to stay in hiding in Delaware for several months before finally finding her way into Pennsylvania. She would eventually be reunited with her husband in Canada.

TESTIMONY
Who Could You Trust?

The former slave Anthony Dawson was interviewed during the Depression years by writers working with the Federal Writers' Project. As a slave in North Carolina, he had seen first-hand how hard it was to decide who could be trusted along the Underground Railroad, and who could not. This is from *When I Was*

a Slave: Memoirs from the Slave Narrative Collection.
(The word *Sesesh* here is a shorthand term describing
people with pro-secessionist, pro-slavery sentiments.)

Dat was de way it worked. Dey was all kinds of
white folks just like dey is now. One man in
Sesesh clothes would shoot you if you tried to run
away. Maybe another Sesesh would help slip you
out to the underground and say "God bless you,
poor black devil," and some of dem dat was poor
would help you if you could bring 'em somethin'
you stole, like a silver dish or spoons or a couple
big hams.

I couldn't blame them poor white folks, with
the men in the War and the women and children
hungry. The niggers didn't belong to them nohow,
and they had to live somehow.

But now and then they was a devil on earth,
walking in the sight of God and spreading iniquity
before him. He was de low-down Sesesh dat
would take what a poor runaway nigger had to
give for his chance to get away, and den give him
'structions dat would lead him right into de hands
of de patrollers and get him caught or shot.

Yes, dat's de way it was. Devils and good people
walking in de road at de same time, and nobody
could tell one from t'other.

CONNECTIONS

- The story of the near-fatal injury suffered by a young Harriet Tubman while living in the Bucktown area is in Chapter 10.
- In the wake of the Dover Eight escape, authorities would soon show up at the home of a suspected station master, Rev. Samuel Green. That story is in Chapter 11.
- Tubman's father, Ben Ross, would come under suspicion as well. That story is in Chapter 15.

TRAVEL RESOURCES

The Dover Green is part of the **First State Heritage Park**, which offers a regular slate of walking tours and other events that will be of interest to history buffs.

- The name of the street where the park's welcome center is located has changed in recent years. That address is currently 121 Martin Luther King Jr. Boulevard North, but it may be easier to find in Google Maps under the old name, 121 Duke of York Street. Both addresses are in Dover, Delaware.
- DEStateParks.com/park/first-state-heritage; 302.739.9192

The broader Dover area is chock full of interesting little museums, as well as shops, restaurants, and other stops. Information about where to go and what to do while there is available from **Kent County Tourism**.

- VisitDelawareVillages.com; 302.734.4888

The **Harriet Tubman Underground Railroad Byway** runs through both Dorchester and Caroline counties in Maryland and then on into Delaware.

- Maryland: HarrietTubmanByway.org; Facebook.com/HarrietTubmanByway; 410.228.1000
- Delaware: TubmanBywayDelaware.org

30: The Flight of Sam And Emeline Hawkins

Middletown and New Castle, Delaware

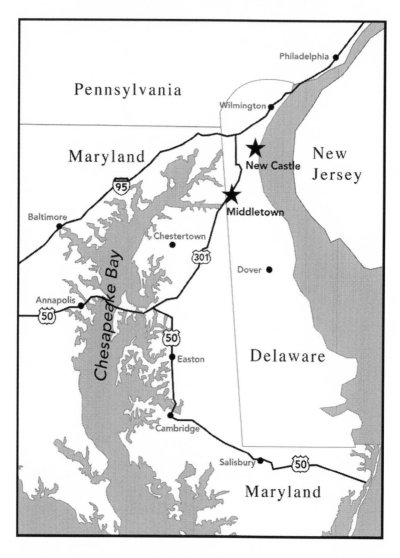

BIG PICTURE
Redemption Song

One thing I've learned in working on this book is that the stories of the Underground Railroad in the Delmarva region often take unexpected twists and turns. The writer and comedian Bertice Berry learned a similar lesson while exploring her African American roots in Delaware.

As a young sociologist at the turn of the 21st century, she wrote a novel called *Redemption Song* about a modern-day bookstore owner who comes across an old slave narrative. There were snippets of Berry's own family history in that fictional narrative—it touched on the story of a white man named John Hunn.

Berry had ancestors who worked on Hunn's farm in the 1800s. Not all that much was known about Hunn at the time she was writing the novel, and she assumed judging by the broad outlines of history we all learn in school that he must have been a "plantation" owner and that her ancestors must have been his slaves. She portrayed her fictional Hunn as the personification of evil.

> Old man Hunn wasn't so old then. He was out hunting my mama and me. He wasn't a real catcher. Others caught slaves for money. He caught 'em for keeps.

When she shared a draft of that novel with her mother, Berry got a little pushback. Her mother had memories of elders in her own childhood telling her that Hunn had been a "good man." Berry didn't buy it. She figured her mother had misremembered things.

In the years that followed, historians in Delaware managed to bring to light the full story of Hunn's work as a conductor on the Underground Railroad. Those historians did not have an easy job of it. While on his deathbed, Hunn had asked his family to destroy all the papers having to do with his work helping slaves. He insisted that he didn't care one whit about what historians and writers might think of him after he was gone.

> I ask no other reward for any efforts made by me in the cause than to feel that I have been of use to my fellow men.

One day, Bertice Berry found herself in front of a TV showing a documentary detailing some of that new research about John Hunn. She was stunned to learn that the man she had portrayed as the personification of evil was actually closer to the opposite. Later, she would learn that those ancestors of hers who had worked on Hunn's farm did so not as slaves, but as free black laborers. She told a journalist:

> It was a shock. I've used this man's name, who was the southernmost conductor on the

Underground Railroad, who remained hidden, the same way we do with everything—we think everything is black and white, good and evil, sin and righteous. You know, no! No.... There's so much more to every story if you just look a little further.

The story of Berry's discovery about Hunn is central to another of her books, *The Ties That Bind: A Memoir of Race, Memory and Redemption.*

STORY
The Flight of Sam And Emeline Hawkins

The Hawkins cabin must have been a boisterous affair. Sam and Emeline had six children living in their place in Ingleside, which remains today what it was in slavery times, a tiny hamlet in the midst of a wide expanse of farm country in the eastern reaches of Queen Anne's County, Maryland, near the Delaware border.

The 1840 census lists all of the Hawkinses as free blacks, but that was a record-keeping mistake, actually. Sam was the only legally free member of the family. He had been born into slavery in 1808, then manumitted to free status later on. During the 1840s, he was making his living through some sort of sharecropper-like arrangement.

Emeline was 15 or so years younger than Sam. She had been a slave of the Glandings family from birth up through the early years of her marriage, when she was sold to a woman named Elizabeth Turner. The timing of that sale meant that the two eldest of Sam and Emeline's children belonged to the Glandings, while the four younger ones were the property of Turner.

Sam tried to find a way out of this legal morass, making several offers over the years to buy the freedom of his wife and some or all of his children. But he had given up hope on that front by 1845. Late that year, he got word to a free black Underground Railroad conductor named Samuel D. Burris that he and his family were ready to make a run for freedom.

Burris showed up at their cabin somewhere around Christmastime and then led the Hawkinses on a northeasterly journey, perhaps shadowing today's Route 301, up to Middletown, Delaware. Most people know Middletown today as a giant collection of big-box stores out on the highway, but it has a pretty, historic downtown section as well.

Another conductor and station master, the Quaker John Hunn, had a 200-acre farm on the outskirts of town. He probably guessed what was up when he saw a covered wagon approaching shortly after sunrise on December 27. Who but runaways would be traveling through a winter's night while six inches of snow were falling?

Burris handed Hunn a letter of introduction from a mutual friend. Inside the farmhouse, the Hunn family got busy stoking the fire and making a big breakfast. Their guests were all suffering from frostbite to one degree or another.

"One man, in trying to pull his boots off, found they were frozen to his feet," Hunn recalled in a written account of the affair that he later sent to the Underground Railroad chronicler William Still.

A suspicious neighbor mucked up the works that morning, sending word to a local constable about the strange goings-on at the Hunn farm. That constable soon arrived at the farm with a pair of slave catchers who started showing off an advertisement offering a $1,000 reward for the capture of members of the Hawkins family.

The constable asked Hunn for permission to search the farm. Hunn was in the midst of demanding that the constable go get the equivalent of a modern-day search warrant when Sam Hawkins bolted out of his hiding spot in the barn and made a run for some nearby woods. The ensuing chase ended with Sam brandishing a butcher knife, the constable pointing a gun, and Hunn pleading with both men to put down their weapons.

When things calmed down, Sam pulled out the identification papers that proved he was a free man. The constable decided to take Sam into town and have a magistrate review the documents. While waiting on the magistrate, Sam got to talking with one of the two slave catchers.

William Hardcastle "put his arm very lovingly around" Sam's neck and drew him into conversation, offering to let Emeline and the four younger children go if Sam would only hand over the two oldest boys.

Sam went for that deal, asking Hunn to bring his family into town so that he could sort out the details. Hunn was skeptical. He asked Sam if he really believed in the promise made by this bounty hunter.

"I do not think master William would cheat me," Sam replied.

He was wrong. When the family arrived, they were all locked up in the Middletown jail. The magistrate, a man named William Streets, soon wrote up an arrest order and sent everyone off to the jail in New Castle, 18 miles away. The party arrived there at midnight and set about rousting the local sheriff from bed.

Downtown New Castle doesn't look all that different today from the way it did the night the Hawkins family arrived. Boasting a bevy of buildings that date to the late 1700s and early 1800s, it sits on a gorgeous stretch of the Delaware River and makes for a fine afternoon of strolling and shopping.

When the Hawkins family arrived in New Castle back in 1845, they found themselves in the sort of dire situation that usually marked the end of the road on a run for freedom. But Sam and Emeline had better luck than most.

Their first bit of good fortune involved that magistrate back in Middletown. In his later written account, Hunn refers to this judge as "my friend William Streets." The arrest order this "friend" of Hunn's wrote up contained a bunch of obvious mistakes. For example, it included Sam Hawkins as part of a group of escaped slaves, when everyone could see from his papers that Sam was a free man. Was Streets incompetent? Did he write up a bad order on purpose in order to try and give the family time to get away? There is no telling either way.

The sheriff in New Castle took one sleepy-eyed look at the arrest order and declared it invalid. He told the slave catchers they would have to go back to Middletown and get Magistrate Streets to write up a new one.

Here is where things got even more curious. The daughter of this sheriff apparently sent word about the predicament of the Hawkins family to the Wilmington home of Underground Railroad conductor Thomas Garrett, who then raced down to the New Castle courthouse with a lawyer in tow.

A hearing was hastily convened before Delaware's chief justice, James Booth Jr. Interestingly, this judge just so happened to be the son of James Booth Sr., who had been a prominent Delaware lawyer at the time the state approved its constitution. The elder Booth had been a vocal supporter of a failed proposal that would have had that constitution outlaw slavery altogether.

Assuming that the younger Booth shared his father's abolitionist sympathies, that would mean that after getting turned in by one white person and then tricked by another, the Hawkins family had somehow managed to run into five sympathetic white people in a row— Magistrate Streets, the sheriff's daughter, Judge Booth, Thomas Garrett, and Garrett's lawyer.

In the hearing that followed, Judge Booth agreed with Garrett's lawyer that in the absence of a legal detention order—the slave hunters were still trying to run that down from the magistrate in Middletown—the Hawkins family should be released immediately. Sam, Emeline, and the six children were soon en route to Garrett's home in Wilmington. From there, they crossed the border into Pennsylvania, landing eventually in the town of Byberry, which was then the home turf of yet another prominent conductor named Robert Purvis.

Not much is known about what became of the family. Like so many escaped slaves, the Hawkinses changed their name in freedom—they chose the surname of Hackett. Sam died two or three years after the family found freedom. I came across one report about how his two oldest sons signed on as apprentices to local craftsmen, but no other details about what happened to Emeline and the other children. They do seem to have stayed in the Byberry area, however, as the Hackett name has lived on through subsequent generations of blacks living in a neighborhood that is now part of the city of Philadelphia.

POSTSCRIPT
'If Thee Knows a Fugitive ... Send Him to Me'

The Hawkins story doesn't end with the family's arrival in freedom. Their escape had a complicated aftermath that includes a courtroom drama that's quite famous in Underground Railroad circles.

Those slave hunters who were after the Hawkinses did eventually make it back to New Castle with a revised arrest order, but they were too late. Furious, they filed a lawsuit against Garrett and Hunn for their part in knowingly helping slaves escape.

The trial that followed unfolded in a courtroom you can visit today at the New Castle Courthouse Museum. There is an exhibit upstairs there dedicated to the whole of the Hawkins affair.

The trial did not go well for Hunn and Garrett. They had bad luck when it came to the selection of a judge, as the case went before U.S. Supreme Court Justice Roger Taney, who would later become author of the infamous Dred Scott decision ruling that blacks could never be U.S. citizens. They had more bad luck when the jury for the case turned out to be full of slave owners.

The two were found guilty. That jury then went out of its way to impose fines even heavier than what the plaintiffs had asked for.

After the conviction, a sheriff approached Garrett, saying "I hope you will never be caught at this again."

Garrett replied with perhaps the most famous words of his life:

> "Friend, I haven't a dollar in the world, but if thee knows a fugitive who needs a breakfast, send him to me."

Garrett proved true to his word, continuing his work as a conductor for as long as slavery was around and despite the financial troubles he experienced as a result of those heavy fines. The number of slaves Garrett helped during his long career on the Underground Railroad is hard to figure precisely, but it likely reached up over 2,000.

When slavery was finally abolished in Delaware in 1865, a good number of Wilmington blacks made an impromptu procession of gratitude to Garrett's house. They placed him in an open carriage and threw a wreath of flowers over his shoulders. According to one newspaper account,

> It seemed as if the whole colored population of the state was turned loose in Wilmington to celebrate.

John Hunn, too, stayed the course. The fines imposed in that lawsuit forced him to sell his farm in Middletown. He eventually moved to nearby Camden, where he was soon back at work as a conductor. After the Civil War he moved his family to South Carolina to join in a Quaker project to start schools for newly freed blacks there.

He died in 1894 and is buried in the Quaker graveyard in Camden. One of his sons, John Jr., would be elected governor of Delaware in 1901.

TESTIMONY
'Abolition Gold'

The free black conductor Samuel Burris did not get caught up in the Hawkins lawsuit, but he ran into his own bit of trouble in 1847. Convicted of helping a Delaware slave named Marie Matthews try to escape, Burris was sentenced to 10 months in prison, after which he was to be sold into slavery.

His Underground Railroad friends up in Philadelphia tried to come to his rescue, secretly sending an abolitionist, Isaac Flint, down to take part in the auction. Here is how William Still describes what happened next:

> When the hour arrived, the doomed man was placed on the auction-block. Two traders from Baltimore were known to be present; how many others the friends of Burris knew not. The usual opportunity was given to traders and speculators to thoroughly examine the property on the block, and most skillfully was Burris examined from the soles of his feet to the crown of his head; legs, arms and body, being handled as horse-jockeys

treat horses. [Isaac] Flint watched the ways of the traders and followed for effect their example.

The auctioneer began and soon had a bid of five hundred dollars. A Baltimore trader was now in the lead, when Flint, if we mistake not, bought off the trader [by offering him] one hundred dollars [on the side to stop his bidding].

The bids were suddenly checked, and ... a few moments were allowed to pass ere Flint had the bill of sale for his property, and the joyful news was whispered in the ear of Burris that all was right; that he had been bought with abolition gold to save him from going south. Once more Burris found himself in Philadelphia with his wife and children and friends, a stronger opponent than ever of Slavery.

Burris moved west eventually, settling in San Francisco, where he remained active in abolitionist causes. He died in 1863. In 2015, on the 168th anniversary of his conviction, Samuel Burris received an official pardon from Delaware Governor Jack Markell in a ceremony at the New Castle Courthouse.

CONNECTIONS

- The burial sites at Quaker meeting houses of several Delaware conductors and station masters are the subject of a Side Trip in Chapter 31.

TRAVEL RESOURCES

Both books by **Bertice Berry** mentioned in the Big Picture section are available on Amazon. In addition to her work as a writer, Berry also works as a comedian and a lecturer.

- BerticeBerryNow.com

The farm of John Hunn was located near where **Middletown High School** stands today. A few years ago, a student there led a successful effort to get a historic marker installed on school grounds commemorating the work of Hunn and other locals who helped runaway slaves on their way north.

- 120 Silver Lake Road, Middletown, Delaware; 302.376.4141

Information about visiting the historic downtown area of Middletown is available from **Middletown Main Street**.

- MiddletownMainStreet.com; 302.378.2977

The New Castle Courthouse Museum is the site of the Thomas Garrett trial and has an exhibit about the Hawkins family.

- 211 Delaware Street, New Castle, Delaware
- History.Delaware.Gov/museums; 302.323.4453

Information about other things to see and do in New Castle is available from the **City of New Castle**.

- NewCastleCity.Delaware.gov/visiting-new-castle; 302.322.9801

A historic marker in honor of **Samuel Burris** stands in the midst of a stretch of farmland outside of Camden, where Route 10 (Willow Grove Road) meets Henry Cowgill Road. Information about visiting Camden and nearby towns is available at **Visit Delaware Villages**.

- VisitDelawareVillages.com; 302.734.4888

The **Harriet Tubman Underground Railroad Byway** runs through both Dorchester and Caroline counties in Maryland and then on into Delaware.

- Maryland: HarrietTubmanByway.org; Facebook.com/HarrietTubmanByway; 410.228.1000
- Delaware: TubmanBywayDelaware.org

31: SIDE TRIPS: QUAKER GRAVEYARDS

Wilmington, Camden, and Odessa, Delaware

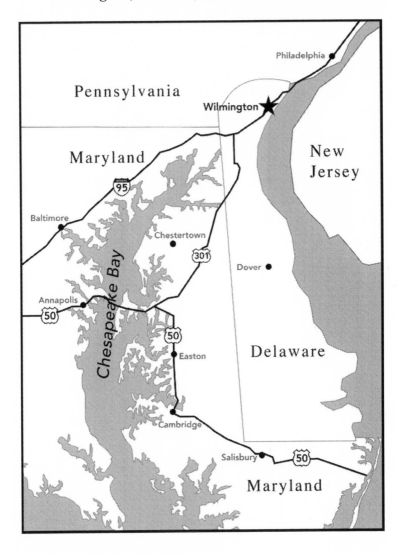

I am a graveyard guy. There is something about wandering aimlessly among tombstones from days gone by that brings me a sense of peace and puts me in a thoughtful frame of mind. Several times while working my way through these journeys to freedom, I went out of my way to stop at old Quaker cemeteries.

The headstones in these places are generally as modest as can be, just oblong slabs laid out in rows, each slab with a name etched into it. There is no distinguishing the richest member of the congregation from the poorest, or the saintliest from the most sinful. The way Quakers see it, we are all equal in death.

That applies even to someone like Thomas Garrett, the Underground Railroad hero who helped some 2,000 people out of bondage and ranked among Harriet Tubman's most trusted confidantes. His stone is just like all the others out back of the Wilmington Friends Meeting House—it took me quite a while to locate his resting place. (Hint: It's over on the 5th Street side of the lot.)

Located in a neighborhood called Quaker Hill, the meeting house here dates to 1817. A couple of earlier meeting houses were here before that. In fact, the congregation dates its history all the way back to 1735.

Set behind a red-brick wall and under a bevy of towering trees, the graveyard has a timeless feel, as if nothing ever changes in the world of the Quakers. The truth, of course, is more complex. In Thomas Garrett's time, for instance, the Quakers were caught up in a tumultuous schism that split the faithful into two competing groups of Friends.

This split is what took Garrett away from his family in Pennsylvania and brought him to Wilmington. Raised in a so-called "Orthodox" home in Pennsylvania, he left there when he decided to sign on with the up-and-coming "Hicksite" sect. These Hicksites placed a premium on personal revelation and downplayed the importance of Scripture. Both sides in the schism felt that slavery was wrong, but the Hicksites tended to embrace a more aggressive, public brand of abolitionism than the Orthodox.

During my visit to Quaker Hill, I tried to imagine what the place looked like on the day of Garrett's funeral in 1871. I have read that the line of people hoping to squeeze into the meeting house that day stretched for more than half a mile out into the surrounding neighborhood.

The conductor John Hunn, who was Garrett's co-defendant in a famous court case involving the flight of Sam and Emeline Hawkins and their children, is buried outside the meeting house in the town of Camden. That meeting house is even older than the one in Wilmington, dating to 1805.

The Appoquinimink Meeting House in the town of Odessa is older still, dating to 1785. It's a tiny little building, set well back from the road. John Hunn came here to worship when he had his farm in nearby Middletown. Local legend has it that the meeting house itself served as a station on the Underground

Railroad—there is apparently quite a convenient-looking hiding place up in the rafters.

I noticed something odd about the graveyard on my visit here. There are two separate cemeteries at Appoquinimink, with one batch of graves set off to the side and behind a brick wall. When I got home, I hopped on my computer and went searching for a little background.

It's a sad story, actually. It seems that the Hicksite-Orthodox split grew so intense here at one point that some Hicksites decided to uproot the dead bodies of some Orthodox brethren and rebury them off in a segregated section of the yard, away from the "true" Hicksite believers. As noble as the overall Quaker dedication to abolitionism back in slavery times can look today, it seems that at least some of those very same Quakers were as capable of flying into crazy rages as the rest of us fallible humans.

TRAVEL RESOURCES

The **Wilmington Friends Meeting House** is at 401 North West Street in the Quaker Hill neighborhood of Wilmington, Delaware.
- WilmingtonDEFriendsMeeting.org; 302.652.4491

The **Camden Friends Meetinghouse** is at 122 East Camden Wyoming Avenue in Camden, Delaware.
- CamdenQuakers.org; 302.698.3324

The **Appoquinimink Meeting House** in Odessa, Delaware doesn't seem to have a proper street address. It's on Main Street (Route 299), just west of the intersection with Route 13. The website and phone number here are for the Wilmington Friends, who help manage the property.

- WilmingtonDEFriendsMeeting.org (click on "Friends in Odessa"); 302.652.4491

The **Harriet Tubman Underground Railroad Byway** runs through both Dorchester and Caroline counties in Maryland and then on into Delaware.

- Maryland: HarrietTubmanByway.org; Facebook.com/HarrietTubmanByway; 410.228.1000
- Delaware: TubmanBywayDelaware.org

32: 'Glory to God! One More Soul Got Safe!'

Wilmington, Delaware

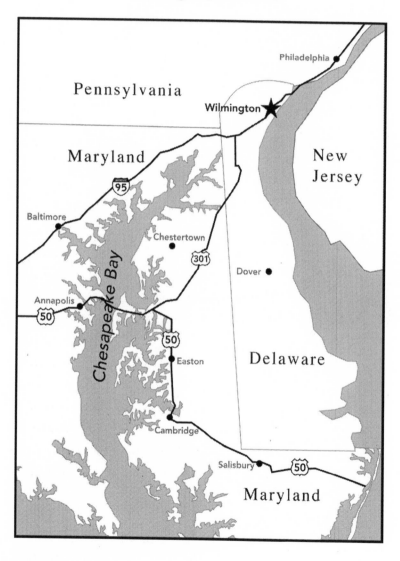

BIG PICTURE
Should I Stay or Should I Go?

Looking back with 21st-century eyes, this question can seem a no-brainer. Who would choose a life in slavery? Who *wouldn't* make a run for it?

We mainly hear nowadays about the slaves who chose to run. They're the ones celebrated in school lessons and books like this. But lots of enslaved people elected to stay put and live out their lives in bondage, even when given a chance to run. The question of why lies at the heart of this story, in which Rachel Ross makes one decision and Josiah Bailey makes another.

In an audio book I listened to, the author of a history of this time period tried to set up the choices facing slaves as they considered escaping. The run-for-freedom side of the ledger in that book was all hope and possibility, while the stay-in-slavery side was all brutality and forced ignorance.

I think that's too simplistic. Yes, life in slavery tended to be filled with cruelty and hardships, but that's not *all* there was. The lives of slaves were also filled with the miraculous stuff of the human heart—love and joy and faith and fellowship. Slaves felt the bonds of family just as surely as any free person—the hardships that they endured together may even have strengthened those bonds.

Making a run for freedom often meant walking out on parents, spouses, and children. Sometimes, it meant worse than that: The owners of successful runaways often punished the family members left behind, selling off parents or siblings or sons or daughters to faraway plantations.

Consider, too, the risk of failure. We don't have precise statistics on how many runaways got caught in Underground Railroad times, but there is no doubt that it was a big number. The punishments inflicted in such cases were often brutal—the accounts in slave narratives about the whipping sessions involved can make your stomach turn. Failed runaways, too, were often sold off into the Deep South.

Should I stay or should I go? The question was anything but a no-brainer.

STORY
'Glory to God! One More Soul Got Safe!'

This is a story about two souls, actually, but that headline is quite correct. Only one soul will get safe in the end, and that's the one belonging to a man named Josiah Bailey. The other soul at the center of this story is Rachel Ross, one of Harriet Tubman's sisters.

Pretty little Tubman-Garrett Park in downtown Wilmington is as good a place as any to think about these two people and the decisions they made. The Christina River, which runs along the park here, was a sort of tipping point on the journey to freedom in slavery days.

This river was the last major geographic hurdle runaways had to get over before they crossed into

Pennsylvania and arrived at Philadelphia, a city that was both big enough and filled with enough anti-slavery activists to offer genuine safe harbor.

A Philadelphia abolitionist found himself in conversation one day with a frustrated slave master, who summed things up this way:

> There is no use in trying to capture a runaway slave in Philadelphia. I believe the devil himself could not catch them [once they] get here.

Tubman-Garrett Park, then, is where the odds of success turned in favor of the runaway. From the edge of the river, you can see the modern-day incarnation of the Market Street bridge off to the right. It's a structure that looms large in the story of Josiah Bailey's run for freedom.

Josiah was not on Harriet Tubman's radar when she set out for the Eastern Shore in the fall of 1856. She was coming to carry her sister, Rachel, out of slavery.

Tubman had eight siblings in all. By this point, she had already helped four brothers make their way to freedom. Three of her four sisters were beyond reach, having been sold off to the Deep South years before. That left Rachel, the last of the Ross children still in slavery on the Eastern Shore of Maryland.

We have no record of what Rachel looked like. Her master never needed to take out a newspaper ad describing her appearance and offering a reward for her capture. She never made it to William Still's place in

Philadelphia, where the meticulous keeper of Underground Railroad records might have jotted down his impressions about the sort of woman she was.

All we know is that Rachel said no. We don't even know how she and Harriet communicated. Could they have met in person? More likely, they exchanged messages through the Underground Railroad grapevine.

Family loomed large in Rachel's decision. Her two children were off living on some other farm when Harriet arrived. Perhaps they had been hired out in routine fashion. Or perhaps their owner, knowing that five of Rachel's siblings had already run away, separated mother from children in order to make it harder for Rachel to run.

There is no telling what was in Harriet Tubman's heart when she got word of Rachel's refusal. But Tubman was never one to wallow for very long in disappointment. If she had to go back north without her sister, she might as well take some other slaves out of bondage while she was at it.

We do know what Josiah Bailey looked like. He stood 5 feet, 10 inches tall. His skin was the color of chestnuts, his head was bald, and he had a scar on his cheek. That scar was probably on the left side, though Joe's owner could not remember for sure. William Still found Joe to be a "civil," "polite" man, blessed with "good common sense" and "well-qualified" to serve as a leader.

Everyone called him "Joe." In slavery, Joe was something of a rock star. Through most of the early 1850s his owner had hired him out to a timberer and farmer named William Hughlett. Hughlett had a pretty big operation at Jamaica Point, which is just up the Choptank River from Cambridge, but on the Talbot County side. By serving as an overseer for perhaps as many as 40 slaves, Joe saved Hughlett the considerable extra expense of hiring a white man for the job.

Joe was so valuable that Hughlett eventually agreed to buy him for the exorbitant price of $2,000. There are a couple different versions about why Hughlett whipped Joe Bailey shortly after making this purchase. One involves punishment for a minor dispute with another slave over a few dollars. The other portrays the whipping as part of a cruel game Hughlett liked to play in order to show his new slaves who the boss was.

Joe pleaded with Hughlett that day: "Habn't I always been faithful to you?"

Hughlett agreed, telling Joe that he had proven himself a "good nigger" and a hard worker.

> But the first lesson my niggers have to learn is that I am master ... [and] so the first thing they've got to do is to be whipped.

Joe took that whipping, but something snapped inside of him amid the pain and humiliation. Getting dressed to go back to work afterwards, he vowed to make sure he would never have to endure another whipping.

"Dis is de last," he told himself.

As the manager of a timbering operation, Joe had lots of connections with blacks whose work took them up and down the rivers of the Eastern Shore and into the big cities beyond the region. He had no doubt heard about the Underground Railroad. He had heard, too, about the woman with a growing reputation as a modern-day Moses. Shortly after that whipping, Joe commandeered a boat and sailed up the Choptank to Poplar Neck, where Harriet Tubman's father, Ben Ross, had a cabin. He asked Ben to tell Harriet that he was ready.

It was thanks to Rachel's decision to stay that Joe got his chance to go. He brought along a brother, William Bailey, who had also endured a recent whipping. Two others, Peter Pennington and Eliza Manokey, joined the party as well.

This is where that Joe-Bailey-as-rock-star business started to work against them. Just as Hughlett had paid an extraordinary price to buy Joe, he now offered an extraordinary reward for his capture, $1,500. That made this party priority number one for pretty much everyone in the business of catching runaway slaves.

The journey to Wilmington usually took a few days. This time, it took a couple of weeks. Tubman used every conducting trick she knew. She split up the runaways, stashing them individually in different safe houses for days a time. At one point, Joe and his fellow runaways were hiding in potato holes while slave catchers passed within a few short yards.

Their progress was laborious—through East New Market, onto Poplar Neck, and then into Delaware, into Sand Town and Willow Grove and Camden and Dover and Smyrna and Blackbird. Finally, they made it to Wilmington, only to find themselves stuck on the wrong side of that last geographical obstacle, the Christina River. Slave hunters were gathered like a flock of vultures at the Market Street bridge.

Tubman sent out calls for help through the Underground Railroad grapevine, and word of her troubles soon made their way to her trusted compatriot, the conductor Thomas Garrett. He was the one who devised an ingenious plan to get the runaways over the river.

One morning in late November, a team of black bricklayers made their way in a wagon across the bridge from north to south. They made quite the raucous display of themselves, singing and shouting all the way, seemingly en route to another day of manual labor.

That evening, they returned, crossing the bridge from south to north and repeating the same raucous display of singing and shouting. No one thought to search the wagon where Joe Bailey and his fellow runaways lay hidden under the stacks of bricks.

When they finally arrived at the Philadelphia home of William Still, he recorded a few details from the interviews with the runaways. Those notes included this tidbit about Joe Bailey:

Although a married man, having a wife and three children (owned by Hughlett), [Joe] was not prepared to let his affection for them keep him in chains—so Anna Maria, his wife, and his children Ellen, Anna Maria, and Isabella, where shortly widowed and orphaned by the slave lash.

Rachel stayed with her children. Joe left his children behind. That's why this story always leaves me pondering the question posed up near the top here: Should I stay, or should I go?

There is one more interesting turn to the story of Joe's escape. Tubman said later that Joe's good spirits and leadership qualities were on display through all of the complications, detours, and near misses this party endured on the way up to Philadelphia. His voice was always "the loudest and the sweetest" of the runaways, she recalled.

Joe thought he had reached his goal by making it into Pennsylvania. But he was wrong. The next stop on the party's journey was New York City, and there the mere sight of Joe Bailey caused one white Underground Railroad activist to exclaim, "I am glad to see the man whose head is worth fifteen hundred dollars!"

This man had recognized Joe from the description on Hughlett's reward posters, which were apparently on display all the way up in New York. The news that he was still being hunted, all these hundreds of miles away from home and in a free state, shook Joe to the core.

He asked how far it was to the Canadian border, and someone showed him on a map. At the sight of all the ground he still had to cover on the road to freedom, Joe sank into a deep depression. Here is how Tubman described the change:

> From that time Joe was silent. He sang no more; he talked no more; he sat wid his head on his hand, and nobody could [a]rouse him or make him take [interest] in anything.

Even as they reached the bridge that would take them into Canada, Joe remained morose. Tubman urged him at one point to take a moment to admire the sight of Niagara Falls, but Joe refused. Finally, as the train they were aboard crossed over the crest of the bridge and made the official crossing into Canada, Tubman managed to shake Joe out of his depression.

> Joe, you're in Queen Victoria's dominions! You're a free man!

Joe's head came up at last. He began to cry. He cast his eyes toward heaven.

> Glory to God and Jesus too! One more soul got safe!

Soon, he was singing and shouting. And repeating:

Glory to God and Jesus too! One more soul got safe!

As he got off of the train, a small crowd of white people gathered around him, some apparently moved to tears by the depth of his joy. One woman reached out to Joe with a handkerchief so that she might help wipe away a few of his tears. Joe had one more joyous shout in him that day:

Only one more journey for me now, and dat is to Hebben!

TESTIMONY
'The Hour Was Come'

James William Charles Pennington was born a slave on the Eastern Shore of Maryland. When James was four, he and his family were given away by their owner to his son as a wedding gift. James and his family soon moved with that new owner to Hagerstown, in Western Maryland, where James would eventually learn the blacksmithing trade.

He was 19 years old when he decided to make a run for it. Later, after becoming a famous orator and minister, he would recall the jumble of things that went through his mind the day he made that decision. This is from his autobiography, *The Fugitive Blacksmith or, Events in the History of James W. C. Pennington,*

*Pastor of a Presbyterian Church, New York, Formerly
a Slave in the State of Maryland, United States.*

It was in the month of November, somewhat past
the middle of the month. It was a bright day, and
all was quiet. Most of the slaves were resting
about their quarters; others had leave to visit their
friends on other plantations, and were absent. The
evening previous I had arranged my little bundle
of clothing, and had secreted it at some distance
from the house. I had spent most of the forenoon
in my workshop, engaged in deep and solemn
thought.

It is impossible for me now to recollect all the
perplexing thoughts that passed through my mind
during that forenoon; it was a day of heartaching
to me. But I distinctly remember the two great
difficulties that stood in the way of my flight: I
had a father and mother whom I dearly loved. I
had also six sisters and four brothers on the
plantation.

The question was, shall I hide my purpose from
them? Moreover, how will my flight affect them
when I am gone? Will they not be suspected? Will
not the whole family be sold off as a disaffected
family, as is generally the case when one of its
members flies? But a still more trying question
was, how can I expect to succeed? I have no
knowledge of distance or direction. I know that

Pennsylvania is a free state, but I know not where its soil begins, or where that of Maryland ends? ...

With such difficulties before my mind, the day had rapidly worn away; and it was just past noon. One of my perplexing questions I had settled—I had resolved to let no one into my secret; but the other difficulty was now to be met. It was to be met without the least knowledge of its magnitude, except by imagination.

Yet of one thing there could be no mistake, that the consequences of a failure would be most serious. Within my recollection no one had attempted to escape from my master; but I had many cases in my mind's eye, of slaves of other planters who had failed, and who had been made examples of the most cruel treatment, by flogging and selling to the far South, where they were never to see their friends more. I was not without serious apprehension that such would be my fate.

The bare possibility was impressively solemn; but the hour was now come, and the man must act and be free, or remain a slave forever. How the impression came to be upon my mind I cannot tell; but there was a strange and horrifying belief, that if I did not meet the crisis that day, I should be self-doomed—that my ear would be nailed to the door-post forever.

The emotions of that moment I cannot fully depict. Hope, fear, dread, terror, love, sorrow, and deep melancholy were mingled in my mind together; my mental state was one of most painful distraction. When I looked at my numerous family—a beloved father and mother, [my] brothers and sisters, &c.; but when I looked at slavery as such; when I looked at it in its mildest form, with all its annoyances; and above all, when I remembered that one of the chief annoyances of slavery, in the most mild form, is the liability of being at any moment sold into the worst form; it seemed that no consideration, not even that of life itself, could tempt me to give up the thought of flight. And then when I considered the difficulties of the way—the reward that would be offered—the human blood-hounds that would be set upon my track—the weariness—the hunger—the gloomy thought, of not only losing all one's friends in one day, but of having to seek and to make new friends in a strange world.

But, as I have said, the hour was come, and the man must act, or forever be a slave.

CONNECTIONS

- The Joe Bailey here is almost certainly the same "Joseph Baily" mentioned in a letter from Sam Green Jr. to his father, the Rev. Samuel Green. The story of that letter is in Chapter 11.
- Harriet Tubman would make at least one more attempt to bring her sister Rachel out of bondage. That story is in Chapter 9.

- The Rev. Pennington quoted here in the Testimony section is the same Rev. Pennington who conducted the marriage ceremony of Frederick Douglass shortly after his escape to freedom. That story is in Chapter 28.

TRAVEL RESOURCES

Be sure to check out the dramatic sculpture of Thomas Garrett and Harriet Tubman that's in the middle of **Tubman-Garrett Riverfront Park**. It's by the artist Mario Chiodo.

- Corner of Water and South French streets, Wilmington, Delaware
- 302.425.4890

There are two places to turn to for information about other things to see and places to go in Wilmington.

- **Riverfront Wilmington:** RiverfrontWilm.com; 302.425.4890
- **Wilmington and Brandywine Valley Tourism:** VisitWilmingtonDE.com; 800.489.6664

The **Harriet Tubman Underground Railroad Byway** runs through both Dorchester and Caroline counties in Maryland and then on into Delaware.

- Maryland: HarrietTubmanByway.org; Facebook.com/HarrietTubmanByway; 410.228.1000
- Delaware: TubmanBywayDelaware.org

Don't Forget the Bonus Materials

Thank you so much for spending some time with this book. I hope that you enjoyed it and that it inspires you to get out and explore the Delmarva Peninsula.

I have prepared some bonus materials and loaded them up on the Secrets of the Eastern Shore website for you to download. These materials can be found at:

SecretsoftheEasternShore.com/tubman-extras

The materials include:

AFRICAN AMERICAN HISTORY SITES

The Delmarva Peninsula is full of sites that speak to the African American experience but are not related to the Underground Railroad. This download lists and describes dozens of those sites in the same geographic region as the book covers—the middle and upper parts of the Eastern Shore of Maryland, and the upper half of the state of Delaware, plus the Seaford area of Southern Delaware.

DETAILED DRIVING DIRECTIONS

Each chapter in this book begins with a visual geographic overview of where the story at hand is situated on or near the Delmarva Peninsula. Where possible, each chapter also includes addresses that can be plugged into your favorite device for generating maps and directions.

I learned in doing my previous book that there are a good number of people who don't like using those devices. For those readers, I have prepared a detailed set of driving directions that begins at Chapter 1 and runs in order from site to site through Chapter 32.

Again, you can download these materials at: SecretsoftheEasternShore.com/tubman-extras

ABOUT THE AUTHOR, ARTIST, & DESIGNER

THE AUTHOR

Jim Duffy lives in Cambridge with his wife, the photographer Jill Jasuta, and whatever collection of cats Jill has assembled at any given moment. As far as the author is concerned, the patience and support Jill exhibited during the writing of this book add up to grounds for sainthood.

For most of the past 20 years, Duffy has been a self-employed magazine writer. He first learned the journalism game as an undergrad at the great Roosevelt University in Chicago. In 2015 Duffy launched Secrets of the Eastern Shore, a business built around helping people explore and celebrate the culture, history, and beauty of the Delmarva Peninsula. (In case you don't know, that word *Delmarva* comes from shorthand references to the three states that govern different parts of the peninsula—Delaware, Maryland, and Virginia.)

Duffy also wrote the first Secrets of the Eastern Shore Guide book in this series. It's titled, *Eastern Shore Road Trips: 27 One-Day Adventures on Delmarva*. There are lots of fun Eastern Shore products and stories on his website and Facebook page. Check them out here:

- SecretsoftheEasternShore.com
- Facebook.com/SecretsoftheEasternShore

THE ARTIST

The front and back covers of this book feature original artwork by Lisa Krentel of Cambridge, Maryland. Born in Brazil, Lisa moved with her family to the United States at the age of 12. She received an MFA from Moore College of Art in Philadelphia. She has worked at various points in her professional life in the fields of publishing, printing, and promotions.

Early on in her artistic journey, Lisa's paintings were inspired by photos she took of underwater scenes while working as a dive master. She now paints in a wide array of different styles. Since moving to the Eastern Shore in 2007, Lisa's work has appeared in a number of regional galleries, museums, and stores. You can occasionally find her volunteering at the little Harriet Tubman Museum and Educational Center in downtown Cambridge.

THE DESIGNER

In addition to being a photographer, the aforementioned Jill Jasuta is a writer and a graphic designer. She designed the cover of this book, as well as the maps that appear inside. She is a graduate of Loyola University Maryland.

- Facebook.com/JillJasutaPhotography
- Jill's photography is also featured prominently at SecretsoftheEasternShore.com.

A Few of My Favorite Sources

CONTEMPORARY BIOGRAPHIES & HISTORIES

- *Bound for Canaan: The Epic Story of the Underground Railroad* by Fergus M. Bordewich
- *Frederick Douglass* by William S. McFeely
- *Harriet Tubman: Bound for the Promised Land* by Kate Clifford Larson. (**NOTE: If you can read just one book about Harriet Tubman, this biography is the one to pick.**)
- *Harriet Tubman: Imagining a Life* by Beverly Lowry
- *Harriet Tubman: The Life and the Life Stories* by Jean M. Humez
- *Harriet Tubman: The Road to Freedom* by Catherine Clinton
- *'Myne Owne Ground': Race and Freedom on Virginia's Eastern Shore 1640-1676* by T.H. Breen and Stephen Innes

- *Runaway Slaves: Rebels on the Plantation* by John Hope Franklin and Loren Schweninger
- *Slave and Free on Virginia's Eastern Shore* by Kirk Mariner
- *Young Frederick Douglass: The Maryland Years* by Dickson J. Preston

PERIOD BIOGRAPHIES & AUTOBIOGRAPHIES

- *Harriet, The Moses of Her People* by Sarah Bradford
- *Life and Times of Frederick Douglass* by Frederick Douglass
- *My Bondage and My Freedom* by Frederick Douglass
- *Narrative of the Life of Frederick Douglass, An American Slave* by Frederick Douglass **(NOTE: If you can read just one book about Frederick Douglass, this autobiography is the one to pick.)**
- *Scenes from the Life of Harriet Tubman* by Sara Bradford
- *The Underground Railroad: A Record of Facts, Authentic Narratives, Letters, &C. Narrating the Hardships, Hair-Breadth Escapes and Death Struggles of the Slaves in Their Efforts for Freedom, as Related by Themselves and Others, or Witnessed by the Author* by William Still

SLAVE NARRATIVES

- *The Classic Slave Narratives* (autobiographies by Olaudah Equiano, Mary Prince, Frederick Douglass, and Harriet Jacobs) edited by Henry Louis Gates, Jr.
- *The Fugitive Blacksmith or, Events in the History of James W.C. Pennington, Pastor of a Presbyterian Church, New York, Formerly a Slave in the State of Maryland, United States* by James W.C. Pennington
- *Life of Isaac Mason as a Slave* by Isaac Mason
- *Slave Narratives: A Folk History of Slavery in the United States, From Interviews with Former Slaves, Maryland Narratives,* by the Federal Writers' Project of the Work Projects Administration
- *Slave Narratives: A Folk History of Slavery in the United States, From Interviews with Former Slaves, Virginia Narratives,* by the Federal Writers' Project of the Work Projects Administration
- *When I Was a Slave: Memoirs from the Slave Narrative Collection,* edited by Norman R. Yetman